The Day My Island Stood Still

For Mother Nature,

who has never once asked if this was a good time.

Thank you for the lessons, the warnings, the wind, the water, the deadlines,

and the occasional full-body reminder of who is boss.

You have scared me, soaked me, humbled me, and pushed me forward

when I would have preferred a nap.

But somehow, in your loud, inconvenient, dramatic way,

you also bring people together.

Rude.

But you are effective.

THE DAY MY ISLAND STOOD STILL

Table of Contents

∞

Prologue

The First Warning System

The first warning system I ever trusted was a Chihuahua named Peanuts.

Peanuts was Dad's dog, although the rest of us were apparently allowed to live in the house too.

Every night before bed, Dad shared his Pepsi with him, and Peanuts occasionally indulged in popcorn like he was watching late-night television and paying the mortgage.

Dad would even make special trips to McDonald's to get Peanuts a hamburger. I was lucky to get one with fries.

Sometime later in life, I figured out why his name was Peanuts and not Peanut. That dog did not have a small personality. He had opinions, routines, preferences, and the general attitude of a man who expected his chair to be waiting when he got home from work.

Peanuts lived with us in Kettering, Ohio, in a small frame house with a single-car garage, and he was fully convinced he ran the family.

Looking back, he may have been right.

But before the sky ever taught me what fear sounded like, Peanuts seemed to know. Dogs hear things before people do.

Children do too, sometimes.

We just don't always know what we're hearing yet.

I was the third of three girls, an unexpected plot twist that arrived years after my sisters had already established a perfectly acceptable society without me. In their minds, I stole Mom and Dad's attention like it was a felony. They didn't treat me like a baby sister so much as a last-minute amendment.

From the outside, it was an ordinary life.

But inside that house, you learned to read a room the way other kids learned to read books. It was my mother's tone. The footsteps.

The weight of a door closing. The sentence that didn't get said.
Some days the safest place was the hallway.
Some days it was outside.
Sometimes I ran.

Sometimes I stayed.
Back then, adults had the keys. To the house. To the car. To the answers.
Children just learned which rooms felt safe and which ones didn't.
Either way, I got good at surviving whatever came next.

I did not understand storms then.

I only understood sound.

The way a house could groan above you. The way adults got quiet when they
were trying not to scare the children. The way a room could look exactly the
same and still feel changed forever.

Back then, I believed a roof meant safety.

I believed walls knew their job.

I believed grown-ups could explain what was happening if something bad
enough happened.

But that was the first lesson weather ever gave me:
A house can be standing and still fail to protect you.
And sometimes the body knows that before the mind has words for it.
For a long time, I couldn't write any of this without cracking open. I could live
it, survive it, even joke through it—but looking back felt like grabbing live
wire. I stayed angry at the future that got uprooted and twisted into something
I never planned.

But the truth is, the stubbornness didn't come from nowhere.
I come from women who did not back down.

My mother raised three girls in the 1960s and probably did more before
breakfast than most people do in a week. My grandmother milked cows,
slopped pigs, raised children, and still put supper on the table because that was
the job and she did it. My aunts taught me grit in different languages: horses,
swimming, dancing, business, family, faith, country, and the quiet art of
standing back up.

They loved their men.
They raised their children.
They carried more than anyone thought to measure.
They gave everything—sometimes for men, sometimes for children,
sometimes for country, and sometimes because nobody offered them another
script.

Every time I write about them, I cry, not because they were weak, but because they never got to be.

So when I wonder where my stubbornness came from, I do not have to look far.

It was handed down.

Not wrapped in a bow.

More like a cast-iron skillet.

Heavy, useful, and capable of doing damage if necessary.

And now I'm old enough to ask the question

they didn't always have time to ask:

Is it a good trait, being this stubborn?

Is it a bad one?

Does it chase men away, or does it pull the right ones closer?

Is it independence?

Or just survival wearing perfume?

More than eighteen months after Hurricanes Helene and Milton, the fog has lifted just enough for

me to put the pieces in order without bleeding all over the page. I don't want to be angry

anymore. I want to understand what happened and what it made of me.

In Ohio, weather wasn't a forecast so much as a roommate. Winter didn't arrive it moved in,

got comfortable and stayed way past its welcome. Spring showed up like it had to knock first.

Tornado weather was always present, always in the background. Sirens on schedule. Warnings

on TV. The whole town practicing the sound of emergency until it became just another noise.

That was the danger of growing up around warnings.

After a while, even fear starts to sound familiar.

Until the day it doesn't.

I didn't know it then, but Ohio was training me.

Because later, weather wouldn't just be something outside the window. It would become

something I could feel in my skin: pressure shifting, air sharpening, the world holding its breath

before anyone said a word.

The Chihuahua always knew first.

Peanuts was small but mighty.

Before the television warnings.
Before the adults started lowering their voices.
Before the sky turned serious enough for grown people to stop pretending.
Peanuts would stiffen.
Listen.
Tremble.
Bark at nothing we could see.
Except it was never nothing.
And on April 3, 1974, the sky proved it.

Chapter 1
The Sound Before the Words

I learned the sound before I learned the words.
In Ohio, tornado weather was just… there. We practiced hiding under desks or crouching in
hallways with our heads between our legs, like that was a plan. The air-raid horn wailed on its
monthly schedule, and half the town didn't even look up, just kept folding towels and stirring
chili like the siren was a kitchen timer.
On television, there was always that stern weekly interruption too:
"This is a test of the Emergency Broadcast System. This is only a test."
It played so often it became part of the furniture: official, ominous, and somehow ordinary. Something everyone pretended not to hear until the day you actually did.
That's how you know something has become normal.
It can be screaming, and people keep stirring the chili.
In 1974, the grown-ups later called it the Super Outbreak. They said it with a kind of distance,
like naming it made it smaller. Like giving a thing a title meant you could file it away and go
back to dinner.
Super. Outbreak.
Two words that sound almost impressive until you understand what they were trying not to say
out loud: one of those tornadoes was an F5 that erased Xenia, Ohio.
Not damaged.
Not hit hard.
Erased.
I didn't see Xenia with my own eyes, not then. I heard it over the kitchen radio and through
television anchors whose voices had gone tight around the consonants.

I heard the numbers the
way adults say numbers when they don't want to look directly at what they mean: people dead,
hundreds injured, families gone quiet in the middle of an ordinary Wednesday.
But numbers never show you what isn't there anymore.
We lived in Kettering, maybe thirty miles away. Close enough that the weather felt personal. Far
enough that grown-ups could still tell themselves it was happening to somebody else.
I was maybe twelve years old.

A week earlier, Dad and I had gone to the movies to see *Gone with the Wind*, which felt both educational and extremely long to a kid who mostly wanted popcorn. I remember the velvet seats, the lobby smelling like butter and carpet shampoo, and thinking somewhere around intermission that no one should be allowed to talk that much without taking a break.

Apparently, the universe appreciated the irony.

Back then, there were no spaghetti models. No Doppler radar we could sit and watch like a

movie. No neat little maps showing what might happen next. What I remember isn't a forecast.

It's the moment the air changed.

The light went wrong first, like someone dimmed the whole world. Then came that sharp, wet,

electric smell, the one that makes your stomach tighten before your brain knows why.

My body learned the forecast before the TV did.

Inside the house, everything sounded too loud. A cabinet door. The refrigerator. A shoe on the

floor. Someone speaking in a voice that meant, *don't make this harder than it already is.*

I didn't have the language for what was happening outside or inside.

I just knew the pressure had moved in.

It always moved in before anything broke.

So I did what made sense to a twelve-year-old trying to breathe.

I climbed my tree.

Then I climbed onto the roof.

I didn't ask. I didn't think. I just went.

Behind me, the screen door banged open. Peanuts, our Chihuahua and first official warning

system, stayed safely inside the house but barked like he had been hired by Civil Defense.

"Get down from there!" my mother shouted, sharp enough to cut through the strange hush.

"Right now!"

I didn't answer.

If I answered, I'd have to come down.

And we all know it is better to ask for forgiveness than permission—especially when you're

twelve and already halfway across the shingles.

The roof, ridiculous as it sounds, was the one place where the house couldn't follow me.

The shingles were gritty under my palms. The air had that ozone bite to it, like a warning.

 I scooted until I could put my back against the chimney and still see the whole neighborhood.

The street had gone oddly empty, as if everybody had been called home at once. A trash can

tipped and rolled, slow at first, then faster. Tree branches lifted and trembled without any breeze

to explain it.

Across the street, Edith, our neighbor and, of course, my mother's best friend stood on her porch

with one hand braced on the railing, staring at the sky.

Then she saw me on the roof.

Her eyes widened. She started to lift a hand, then thought better of it, like she didn't want to

startle me off the edge. Her mouth opened not to scream exactly. More like she was deciding

whether to call my name or call my mother.

It landed, finally, in the shape of a prayer.

And then the silence came.

Not quiet silence.

That dead, waiting silence where everything feels like it is holding its breath.

I turned in a slow circle, trying to see all of it at once, trying to understand what kind of sky does

this.

The sky had gone the wrong color. Blackened. Bruised. Heavy. Low enough to make you feel

smaller. It was spinning in places it had no business spinning, like it had forgotten the rules.

Somewhere nearby, the first drops of rain started: fat, cold splats that darkened the shingles. The

grit turned slick. The pitch of the roof felt steeper than it had a minute ago.

They said later that at least a hundred tornadoes dropped out of the sky that day. That's how

adults talk about the unthinkable: *at least*, like the sky had only misbehaved a moderate amount.

But I believed it.

Because what I remember next is the sound.

It wasn't one train.

It was freight trains coming from different directions: a low roar you felt in your chest before

you understood it with your ears. Like the air itself was being pulled apart.

I remember gripping the shingles so hard my fingers hurt. I remember thinking, with the pure

logic of a twelve-year-old

If I can see it, I'll know where it is.

As if watching was the same thing as control.

My mother yelled again, my name this time. It reached me late, warped by the wind.

I shifted my weight to look over the edge, and the wet grit under my palm gave way.

Just a quick slide.

A couple inches of skin and fear.

My stomach dropped so hard it felt like I had swallowed the sky. For one clean second I saw it:

my body rolling, the ground rushing up, my mother's scream turning into a sound

I would never unhear.

I flattened myself to the roof and stayed there, cheek pressed to the rough shingle, breathing in

that wet-electric air like it was a lesson.

The...nothing.

A pause so complete it felt staged.

Then the sound again.

Closer.

Wider.

Everywhere at once.

Then silence again.

The kind that feels louder than the noise did.

I didn't move until I felt the roof stop vibrating under me.

I didn't move until I heard my mother's footsteps under the overhang, hard and purposeful, the

kind of footsteps that meant I was about to learn something the old-fashioned way.

When I finally scooted down to the edge, she reached up and grabbed my wrist like she was

hauling in a fish.

"Inside," she said.

I opened my mouth.

"Inside," she repeated.

Somehow, that one word contained a whole sermon.

By the time my feet hit the ground, the storm had moved on just enough to make her brave. She marched me through the yard with one hand clamped on my arm, and when I tried to angle my body away like I was too big to be manhandled, twelve-year-old dignity and all, her other hand landed on my behind with a firm, efficient smack.

Not angry.

Not theatrical.

Just… administrative.

It said: *Do not climb on roofs in this weather. Do not test me while the sky is testing all of us.*

Edith was still on her porch.

She didn't say a word.

She watched us go, prayer forgotten, and I could tell by her face she was filing this away for

later, because nothing travels faster than tornadoes and best friends.

Inside, the house smelled like damp wood and nerves. The living room lamp flickered once,

twice, like it couldn't decide whether it believed in electricity. Somewhere down the street, a

siren started up, then faded, then started again, searching for the right disaster.

My mother shut the door and slid the lock with a click that sounded too loud.

For a minute we just stood there.

Dad had the TV on low, the meteorologist pointing at nothing useful. My sisters, older, annoyed,

and pretending not to be scared, hovered like they were waiting for permission to act like humans again.

My mother didn't look at me.

She looked past me, toward the windows, and I could see it in her shoulders.

She was counting.

Doors.

Kids. Time.

That was my first real lesson in scale. In power.

In how the sky cadecide to become something

else entirely without asking permission. I didn't have words for it then.

But I learned the sound.

The color.

The pressure.

The strange hush that comes right before the world changes.

And once you learn that, you don't unlearn it.

You just carry it.

A few years later, Ohio taught me a different kind of lesson.

Tornadoes make you look up and listen.

A blizzard makes you stay put and wait, whether you're

ready or not.

Chapter 2
My First Official Hunker

By 1978, I already knew the sky could turn mean.

What I didn't know yet was that it could also trap you in your own house and call it winter.

That was the year I learned the phrase *hunker down*.

"Hunker down" is one of those phrases' adults love to use when things have already gone

sideways. They say it during wars, storms, pandemics, power outages, family arguments, and

probably PTA meetings. It sounds calm and practical, like someone has a plan.

Usually, it means nobody has a plan.

In our house, it meant stay put, don't panic, drip the faucets, play cards, eat grilled cheese, and wait for Ohio to finish throwing its tantrum.

The Blizzard of 1978 was my first official hunker.

I did not receive a certificate.

From January 25th through the 27th, Ohio did what Ohio does when it's feeling dramatic: it turned winter into a full-time job. Adults hadn't invented phrases like

polar vortex yet to make

misery sound scientific.

It was just cold.

Bitter cold.

And then it got worse.

People later called it the worst blizzard in Ohio history. They said fifty-one people died. They said the National Guard had to come in,

the Ohio Turnpike closed, and doctors and nurses

needed rides to work like we had all been dropped into an old pioneer story with better hair.

Those are the facts.

What I remember is the world getting bossy.

Snow takes over without asking. Roads disappear. Cars become decorative. The sky presses
down low and flat, pinning everyone in place. Even sound changes; everything muffled, every noise softened, like the storm is holding a finger to its lips.
Shhh.
Inside, it was just me, Peanuts, and my middle sister, Cindy. Peanuts mostly stayed under the blankets, shivering the way Chihuahuas do, like he had
personally, been betrayed by the temperature.
I was in my teens. Cindy was six years older, which was old enough to think she knew
everything and young enough to still be wrong in exciting ways.
We didn't like each other most of the year, but blizzards have a way of forcing temporary peace
treaties.
Also, we were stuck.
And when you're stuck with someone you don't like, you either kill them or play cards.
We played cards.
We listened to the wind and the radio, music crackling through like it was trying to be cheerful on purpose.

We danced so we wouldn't freeze, because the heater kept clicking on

and off. I swear it was debating early retirement.

The house smelled faintly of wet wool, damp boots, and whatever soup had been reheated for the
third time.
At one point, Cindy opened the freezer and stared into it like she was assessing our odds.
"We have enough food," she announced, as if she were head of the Ohio Emergency
Management Agency.
"We do?" I asked.
She pointed at a frozen loaf of bread and two bags of peas.
That was our long-term plan.
"See?" she said.
This is what I mean when I say we were unqualified.

Still, somehow, we had fun. Real fun. Not the kind where you pretend you're fine because adults are listening. We wrapped ourselves in blankets and watched TV, the screen flickering with weather warnings and bad reception. We ate grilled cheese and canned soup. We drank hot cocoa like we were starring in a wholesome commercial.

And we never even lost electricity, which felt like winning the lottery in mittens.

I honestly don't remember where the rest of the family was. In my memory, it was just me and

Cindy, making a small workable world out of whatever we had.

That's what blizzards do.

They don't have one big moment.

They move in and refuse to leave.

Inside our living room, time slowed down. One white day smudged into the next. There was

nowhere to go and nothing to do but stay in the house and be with each other.

Which, in our family, was always its own kind of weather.

The Blizzard of 1978 taught me one kind of survival:

Stay inside.

Keep warm.

Drip the

faucets. Play

cards.

Wait it out.

That made sense in Ohio.

But not every storm rewards staying put.

I would not understand that until much later, when the weather had water

behind it and bridges

that could close.

Some storms ask for patience.

Some storms ask you to run.

And knowing the difference can become the whole story.

Here's the strange thing: the blizzard made Cindy gentle.

Not all the time. She was still Cindy. Let's not rewrite history just because there was weather.

But there were small, almost accidental moments when her sharpness softened.

One night, we were sitting on the couch, a blanket over both of us like we actually liked each

other. The wind rattled the windows, and the lights flickered once just enough to make my

stomach drop.

Cindy reached over and took my hand.

Not in a dramatic, sister-movie way. Just a quiet squeeze.

Like she was saying, "I'm here. Don't freak out. Not tonight."

And I didn't.

Because even when you don't always like someone, you can still feel safe with them.

After the storm, the world looked like it had been erased and redrawn by someone with no sense

of scale. The drifts were taller than they should have been. The edges of the sidewalks were

gone. Everything familiar was buried under a smooth, bright blankness that made you squint.

My friend Cheryl actually walked over to my house.

We decided this was clearly the perfect time to explore on foot, because teenagers are nothing if

not optimistic and deeply unqualified for weather decisions.

We waded through snow up to our waists and picked icicles six feet long off rooftops like we

were harvesting frozen spears. We stabbed them into snowbanks as if we were planting flags on

conquered territory.

"This is how people die," Cheryl said, laughing.

"Probably," I said.

It was cold, ridiculous, and absolutely perfect in the way only surviving something slightly

stupid can be.

What that storm taught me before Florida, before hurricanes, before grown-up loss, was that

sometimes weather doesn't send you running.

Sometimes it sends you together.

Hunkering down works for blizzards.

It works when the pipes might freeze, when the roads disappear, when the smartest thing you can

do is stay where you are and wait for the world to become passable again.

But five years later, in August of 1983, I did the opposite.

I got married, packed a U-Haul, and went south.

I thought I was leaving Ohio weather behind.

That was adorable.

Florida was waiting with sunshine, palm trees, red tide, humidity, and a whole new set of rules. Ohio had taught me how to stay put.

Florida was about to teach me when to leave.

Chapter 3
The U-Haul Plan

Right after high school, Kevin Sr. and I got married, which is the kind of sentence that sounds either romantic or alarming, depending on who's reading it.

The next year, we received an invitation from his sister,

Brenda, to come join the family in

Florida.

Back then, in 1983, Tampa still felt like the land of opportunity. Paradise, even, if you didn't

look too closely at the humidity, the palmetto bugs, or whatever Florida was doing to people's

hair.

We were young enough to think love and determination counted as a moving plan.

And maybe they do, as long as you don't ask too many practical questions too early.

The main reason we went to Florida was Brenda.

She was already there. She made it sound doable. And when you are young, newly married, and

trying to figure out where your life is supposed to begin, doable can sound a lot like destiny.

Brenda was a woman of faith, but not the kind that made you feel watched or measured or

quietly corrected. She believed in God without using Him as a weapon.

She was steady.

Warm.

Certain in the way some people are when they've decided kindness isn't weakness. It's discipline.

She never judged me.

That matters more than people realize, especially when you're young and newly married and

trying very hard to look like you know what you're doing when, in fact, you are mostly

improvising in clean clothes.

Brenda taught me a lot about being a wife, though not in the sugary magazine-advice way. She

taught me the useful thing, the things that hold when life gets difficult: how to support a

marriage without disappearing inside it, how to help without keeping score, how to speak

plainly, how to stand beside somebody instead of in front of them or behind them.

And she did most of that just by being herself.

At some point, Brenda needed her furniture brought down from Ohio to Florida.

So naturally, because we were young, married, and apparently allergic to doing anything the easy way, we loaded up a U-Haul and moved.

That was the whole plan.

Not five plans.

Not a backup plan.

One.

A truck. Some furniture. Our youth. And the kind of confidence people only have before reality

starts collecting receipts.

I remember the feeling of it more than the details: the heavy lift of furniture, the smell of

cardboard and old wood, the truck-cab vinyl heating up in the sun, the road stretching long in

front of us, Ohio shrinking in the rearview mirror while Florida waited ahead like a dare.

We said goodbye to family and friends the way young people do: quickly, bravely, and without

fully understanding what goodbye costs until much later.

We weren't exactly moving to paradise.

We were moving toward a maybe.

There's a difference.

Paradise is what people sell you in postcards.

A maybe is messier.

A maybe looks like hauling somebody else's furniture across state lines and calling it a future.

Still, Florida felt like a promise: warm, open, and far enough away from everything familiar to

feel like a fresh start.

And Brenda was there waiting on the other end, which made the whole thing less frightening.

That is what family can do when it's good: make risk feel survivable. Make a strange place feel

less strange. Stand at the edge of your new life and wave you in.

I didn't know then that Florida would become the great weather system of my adulthood.

I didn't know it would hand me marriage and motherhood, storms and grief, freedom and loss.

I didn't know how many times I would leave and return, rebuild and begin again.

I only knew we were headed south, and Brenda was part of the reason the road felt possible.

Sometimes that's how a whole life
starts.
Not with certainty.
With a U-Haul.
A young marriage.
Someone waiting at the other end.
And a feeling you can't quite name
yet, something like hope, something
like foolishness. Ithought I was
moving toward warmth.
Ididn't know I was moving toward
water.

Chapter 4
Florida Was Not Myrtle Beach

Florida wasn't completely new to me.
We had met once before, on a family vacation, and she did not make the
best first impression. Before Florida became the great love affair and long
argument of my adult life, it was supposed
to be a vacation.
That was my first mistake.

A few years before the blizzard, back when I was a teenager and my biggest
weather concern
was whether humidity would ruin my hair, my mom announced
we were going to Clearwater, Florida.

Myrtle Beach had been the family standard for years, but apparently she
woke up one day and
chose the Sunshine State.
We didn't ask for an explanation.
In Christian families of the seventies, you didn't ask for explanations.
You got in the car.
Mom and Dad in the front seat.

Me and my sisters in the back, riding my own weather.
I remember looking out the window and feeling oddly alone, like I was
missing something I was
supposed to be doing. My sled was probably still leaning against the garage
back home. My
friends were out there somewhere making a day of the snow while I headed
south with my
parents and whatever mood had settled into the car.

We finally made it over the bridge into Clearwater, and within seconds, the
smell hit us.
Not a bad smell.
Not a dumpster smell.
This was a symphony of death, rot, vegetables, fish, seaweed, and decay, the
kind of smell that
makes you reevaluate your entire belief system.

We stood there gagging and confused while Florida tried to kill us with
odors from the Gulf of
Mexico we did not yet have names for.
Back then, we just called it:

———————— ∞ ————————

Why does the Gulf hate us?
Forty years later, I learned the name.
Red tide.
The strange thing is, it isn't exactly the same now, but it triggers the same gut-
drop. Different
odor, same nervous-system alarm. The kind that drags memories up by the
collar and tells your
body to get ready before your brain has caught up.
And here's the lesson:
When red tide rolls in, you don't hunker down.
You run.
So we did.
We got back in the car and drove to Myrtle Beach like Florida had been a
mistake on the map.
I loved Myrtle Beach.
Myrtle Beach taught me how to body surf, how to hunt for shark teeth like
buried treasure, and
which shells were worth keeping and which ones were just good for throwing
back. Myrtle
Beach was the kind of water you visited. You got sunburned, you laughed,
you rinsed sand out of
places sand should never be, and then you went home.
I've always loved the water.
Even then, I wasn't entirely sure it loved me back.
In the bathtub, I counted how long I could hold my breath underwater like it
was an Olympic
event no one was watching. In the shower, I'd tilt my head up and stare into
the spray like I
could intimidate water into behaving.
At Myrtle Beach, I learned what a wave could really do: tumbling me end over
end, packing my
mouth, nose, and ears with sand and shells as if it were trying to make me part
of the shoreline.
Myrtle Beach lets you borrow the ocean for a week.
Florida moves it in with you.
I didn't know that yet.
Not fully.
Back then, vacation was motel pools, sunburn, and seashells. The pools were
always over-
chlorinated, the sunburn was always underestimated, and the seashells came
home in

Ziploc bags
that smelled like an unregulated aquarium.

That first Clearwater trip should have warned me.

Florida had already shown me who she was: beautiful, humid, slightly

ridiculous, and fully
capable of turning the Gulf into a science experiment with a bad attitude.
I was young.

All I saw were beaches and seafood buffets.

I didn't know yet that one day Florida would stop being a destination and

become my home and
that home would come with rules, most of them written by weather.
Years later, I came back to Florida on purpose.

Not as a kid on a family trip.

As a wife with a U-Haul, a future I hadn't stress-tested yet, and a sister-in-law

named Brenda
waiting at the other end.
Florida stopped being a vacation and became my address.

I learned my way around grocery stores with palm trees in the parking lot. I
learned that
humidity was not weather so much as a personal relationship.

I learned that paradise had traffic,
bugs, and a way of making your hair surrender before breakfast.

And then, in 1985, the weather started naming itself like it wanted to make

sure I understood I
hadn't just moved south.
I had moved into a relationship with the sky.

Her name was Elena.

Chapter 5

The Hurricane Party

My first experience with what we would now call spaghetti models was
Hurricane Elena in 1985.
I was twenty-three and had just had my first baby in April, which meant I
was still new enough
to motherhood to believe sleep was optional and panic was a personality
trait.
Kris, my first of three boys, was four months old and still in that blessed
stage of life where his
entire job was to sleep, eat, and poop like it was a sacred routine.

He wasn't aware of hurricanes
or forecasts or grown-up dread. He just did what he needed to do, calmly
and consistently, three
things I would have loved to manage that week.
We were not ready for a hurricane.
To be fair, I was barely ready for diapers and feedings, which turned out to
be the real
emergency. Compared to a newborn, Hurricane Elena felt like background
noise right up until
the weather people started pointing at maps covered in squiggly lines like
they were explaining a
crime scene.
My only coherent thought was:
Are you kidding me?
I had just figured out which end of the baby did what.
Now I was apparently supposed to figure out the wind.
Everyone around us seemed to have opinions. Boards. Coolers. Checklists.
 People said things
like "generator" with the confidence of someone who had owned

one for more than six minutes.
We had a baby and a vague sense of optimism, which, looking back, is not a
hurricane strategy.
Still, Kevin and I decided this might actually be fun. Just the two of us and a
brand-new baby,
tucked inside for a few days while a hurricane did whatever hurricanes do.
Maybe even a nap, if the universe was feeling generous.
Naturally, the first thing we did was go to Blockbuster Video.
Because how can you have a hurricane party without a good movie?

We rushed over like we were preparing for a very damp, very loud film festival.
The plan was simple: stock up on the good stuff, go home, and let this
hurricane party unfold like a cozy, slightly dramatic weekend indoors.
Blockbuster looked like the apocalypse, only with membership cards.
People everywhere.
Crowds.
Pushing.
Shoving.
That wild look in everyone's eyes that says, "If I don't get a movie, civilization
will end."
The shelves were already stripped bare, like locusts had come through with late
fees.
And the sound in there...the jangly doorbell, the customer chatter, the plastic
cases clacking...
made it feel like panic had its own soundtrack.
A man next to us was arguing with his wife about batteries like it was a divorce
topic.
"D-cells," he said, holding up a pack like evidence.
"We need D-cells."
"For what?" she asked.
"For the flashlight!"
"We don't have a flashlight that takes D-cells!"
He stared at her like she had confessed to a crime.

I remember thinking it was funny that he was worried about batteries while we
were renting
movies that required electricity.
Then I looked down at the baby in my arms and thought, "I don't even know
what kind of
batteries my baby takes."
Kris smelled like milk and clean laundry and the soft,
warm sweetness of a creature who
believed the world was reliable.
I kept kissing the top of his head like that could protect him
from the wind.
That was my introduction to Florida storm culture: frantic errands, last-minute
scrambling, and
one truth nobody says out loud until you have lived it:

The cone means nothing.

Not to your nerves.

Not to your plans.

Not to the part of you that just wants someone to point at a map and say, "Here. This is exactly
what will happen."

The lines can wiggle. The forecast can shift. The storm can change its mind. And you still have
to decide what you are going to do.

In that moment, all I knew was that the line at Blockbuster looked like the end times, and I was
holding a baby who still needed to eat every two hours, regardless of meteorology.

I can't remember what movie we hoped to get, but I know this:

It was absolutely not on those shelves.

Not even close.

All that was left were the cinematic leftovers, the kind of movies nobody chooses unless they are
trapped in a house with weather and a newborn.

So we did what reasonable, sleep-deprived new parents would do.

We grabbed something old, something black-and-white, something Cary Grant, and something
else that looked like it might keep us awake.

We threw in a few snacks too, because clearly we were building a survival kit.

At the counter, the clerk looked at our stack and said, "Y'all gonna rewind those, right?" like
rewinding was the last moral obligation left in society.

Kevin laughed too loud.

I laughed because I needed to.

Outside, the air felt thick, like it was holding its breath.

The sky had that too-bright look it gets
before it decides to misbehave. People were loading cars. People were arguing about plywood.

Somebody had a grill going like they were about to barbecue in the parking lot during the
apocalypse.

Florida is nothing if not committed to snacks.

We went home feeling weirdly victorious, like we had outsmarted a
hurricane with popcorn and classic cinema.
Which, if you have ever met a hurricane, is an adorable way to think.
Back at the house, our prep was mostly me walking from room to room
trying to remember what
people said you were supposed to do.
Fill the bathtub?
Why?
Who decided that?
Should I tape the windows?
With what tape?
Diaper tape?
Masking tape?
Faith?

We had a few candles, a radio that may or may not have worked, and enough
diapers to last a
couple of days if Kris continued being the reasonable little person he was. I
lined up baby
supplies like offerings to the Weather Gods.
Kevin checked the flashlight.
I checked the baby.
Again and again, because the baby was the only thing in the house with a
reliable schedule.

That Labor Day weekend, we were spared.
The storm veered.
The wind behaved.
We didn't even lose electricity.
Not a flicker.
Not a dramatic candle moment.
 Nothing.
The world stayed on, and so did the baby.

So those movies we panic-rented turned out to be just fine.

We sat there with our brand-new son, watched our bargain-bin classics, ate our survival snacks, and congratulated ourselves on surviving a hurricane we never actually met.

By Monday, we were refreshed, rested, and completely miseducated.

That was the first little lie a hurricane ever told me.

Because we were fine, we thought it hadn't been serious.

Because the lights stayed on, we thought the warnings had been too much.

Because the worst thing that happened to us was a poor movie selection, we thought we had

understood the storm.

We hadn't.

We had only been lucky.

So we decided hurricanes didn't mean much.

Forecasts were just squiggles.

Weather people liked attention, especially the weatherman wearing suspenders.

We had our movies, our snacks, and a baby who hadn't even noticed the apocalypse that wasn't.

Case closed.

Let's move on.

Except Elena had already done what near misses do.

She let us feel safe without teaching us anything useful.

She let us think we understood the rules when really, we had only been excused from the lesson.

And once Florida knows you'll stay for a near miss, it starts testing what else you'll stay for.

I didn't know it then, standing there with a baby, a bag of videos, and no real hurricane plan.

But the sky was not finished with me.

Not even close.

Chapter 6
The Business of Aftermath

I didn't go to college, unless you count frat parties at the
University of Dayton, and I'm pretty sure MetLife would not have
accepted those credits.
I did graduate high school with high grades that seemed to require
very little effort on my part,
which sounds impressive until you realize I still had no real plan.
I came of age in a strange little crack of American history.
Technically,
 I qualify as a baby boomer, but somehow I missed all the famous
parts.
Too young for Vietnam protests.
Too young when women's liberation was making headlines.
Too young for the energy crisis.
Too young when Nixon being a crook became official instead of
just something people muttered over dinner.
I was too young to make history, but not too young to notice it.

I knew the world felt chaotic. I knew things were unfair. I knew
grown-ups were lying about
how fine everything was.
That part, I understood early.

Maybe that is what eventually drew me toward insurance, the idea
that helping people put
things back together might count for something.
That is the noble version.

The less romantic truth is that it was the only temp job I could
land during the recession in the
1980s.
So no, I did not march into the insurance business with a calling
and a briefcase. I backed into it
because the economy had me by the throat and a temp agency
pointed me toward a desk.

That first temp job was at MetLife, in health insurance.
And by "health insurance," I mean I got to file.
In a room the size of a warehouse.
It was the era of cigarettes and trying to look cool while doing deeply
unglamorous work.

My friend and I would smoke and slide our ashtrays along the tops of the
filing cabinets as we moved down the rows, which was honestly a miracle of
poor judgment and fire-code violation.
It is a wonder we did not burn the place down before lunch.

That phase, thankfully, did not last.
Soon enough, I was hired full-time in Auto and Home Insurance, which
sounded more official
and turned out to be much more consequential.
The training was simple enough: some travel, how to set up a claim, how to
write estimates, how to look at damage and turn somebody's bad day into
paperwork.
Meanwhile, Kevin Sr. held down the fort at home while I learned the
business.
At the time, it all seemed practical.
Straightforward, even.
Here is the form.
Here is the process.
Here is the estimate.
Here is what happens next.
Insurance had its own language.
Date of loss.
Facts of loss.
Coverage.
Deductible.
Estimate.

Depreciation.

Settlement.

The words were useful. They gave chaos a place to stand. They turned disaster
into something

that could be opened, reviewed, assigned, adjusted, and closed.

At least on paper.

But then the phone would ring.

And on the other end was not a file.

It was a person.

A woman who could not find her medicine.

A man who did not know where his dog had gone.

A family sleeping in one room because the rest of the house smelled like wet
insulation and fear.

That was when I began to understand the difference between a claim and a life.

A claim wants documentation.

A life wants mercy.

Somewhere between those two things, I learned that logic may organize damage,
but it does not

heal the person standing in it.

Looking back, I strongly believe the training should have included mental health
maintenance.

Not just how to write a claim.

How to absorb panic without taking it home.

How to listen to people describe the worst day of their lives and still sleep that
night.

How to stay steady when grief comes at you disguised as paperwork.

Because once you have spent enough years in insurance, you realize you are not
really in the business of forms and estimates.

You are in the business of aftermath.

At first, I thought I was learning policies.

I thought I was learning estimates.

I thought I was learning how to put numbers where damage had been.

But what I was really learning was how people sound after the thing they trusted fails them.

A roof.

A wall.

A road.

A town.

A life.

I didn't know it then, sitting at a desk with a phone, a claim file, and whatever confidence I could gather before the next call came in.

But that work was training me too.

Ohio had taught me weather.

Florida had introduced herself.

Insurance taught me the part that comes after.

And in 1992,

Hurricane Andrew was about to make sure I understood the difference.

$$\text{———}\bowtie\text{———}$$

Chapter 7
See XXAL

Seven years and three growing boys later, I thought I understood Florida weather.
Then Andrew hit.

And I found myself on the other side of it, headset on.
I didn't just live through Hurricane Andrew. I worked inside it. Ate inside it. Drank burnt coffee
inside it. Slept inside it, if you can call closing your eyes while phones kept ringing in your head sleep.

Tampa headquarters.
One room.
A dozen young adjusters in a brand-new career we thought we understood.
We had training binders, polite scripts, and the kind of confidence people only have before reality touches them.
Then Andrew touched everything.

We worked twelve to fourteen hours a day, seven days a week, for weeks.
Maybe months.
The days didn't have edges anymore.
They ran together under fluorescent lights and cold air
conditioning, in the constant ringing of phones and the soft hiss of headsets.
Burnt coffee.
Lukewarm fast food. Paper cuts on the same fingers you used to hold the receiver steady while someone on the other end fell apart.

And every morning, as I pulled into the parking lot, there was Snoopy.
MetLife had Snoopy everywhere back then, so there he was: a giant, cheerful cutout popping out of a box, facing the highway like
he was advertising happiness.
He was always there first.
Before my badge swipe.
Before the phones.

Before the day could take shape.
Smiling at traffic. Smiling at the building. Smiling at me.
Same pose.
Same grin.
Like the world was fine.
Some mornings I wanted to thank him for trying. Some mornings I wanted to drag him inside
and make him take calls, because if you're going to smile through a catastrophe, you should at
least earn it.
Inside, the fluorescent lights hit first steady and humming, like a ceiling full of bees you stop
noticing until it is all you can hear. The room was already alive: printers spitting paper, chairs
scraping, headsets hissing, adjusters trying to sound calm while their eyes said otherwise.
Our computer system was fairly new and had a name like it was a coworker. Charlie.
Charlie was supposed to organize the world: policy numbers, losses, notes, outcomes. We wrote
call notes in XXAL, a little secret language that made catastrophe look official. Soon, "See
XXAL" became both instruction and prayer.
Yellow Post-its were everywhere stuck to files, monitors, desk edges. My supervisor's
handwriting showed up again and again like a stamp:
SEE XXAL.

As if anything about this could be contained in a field.
At first, we tried to treat it like work.
Like volume.
Like a backlog you could conquer if you stayed organized.
But catastrophe doesn't behave like a backlog.
It behaves like a tide.
The first real calls came in, and the room changed. Not all at once, but
unmistakably. Less jokng. More Staring at the copier like it would give them an
answer. Some rubbing their temples until their forehead turned pink. Chairs
scraping. File drawers slamming the kind of little violence that shows up when
you don't have anywhere to put the big feelings.

We were trained for losses you could name.
A roof.
A fence.
A car.
We were not trained for the sound of a human voice realizing the world was no longer safe.

The Loop

It settled into a rhythm.

Badge in.

Headset on.

Coffee first, like caffeine could stand between you and disaster.

My supervisor, Kaye, would walk past and drop a file on my desk like it weighed

nothing.

"You good?" she'd ask, the way people do when they already know you're not.

Someone would crack a joke that wasn't funny. Someone would laugh anyway,

because laughter

was still one tool we had left.

Then the phones.

You could hear it before the caller finished their name: the shape of panic in a

breath.

The pause where they decided whether it was okay to cry in front of a stranger.

The small politeness people cling to when everything else is gone.

"Thank you for calling MetLife," I'd say, because the script was what we had.

"How can I help you today?"

As if help was still a simple word.

Andrew was a Category 5. Winds around 165 miles per hour.
 Neighborhoods flattened.
Lives erased.
Those are numbers people recite now.
Back then, they were voices.

A man would talk about his roof like it was a person who had betrayed him.
A woman would apologize before telling you her house was gone, as if losing
your home was an inconvenience you should be sorry for.

Someone would whisper,
"I don't know where to go," and you could hear children in the
background, proof that parenting doesn't pause just because the world stops
behaving.
And sometimes people didn't call about insurance at all.
They called because they needed a witness.

One of the first callers asked me a question I had not been trained to answer.
"How is the insurance man supposed to find us?" he said.
He wasn't being difficult.
He was being literal.
No street signs. No landmarks. Some houses had only one wall standing.
Whole neighborhoods
looked like someone had picked them up, shaken them hard, and put them
back down in the wrong order.

I looked at the form in front of me. At Charlie's blinking cursor. At the neat
little boxes meant for a world that still made sense.
Then I made an executive decision.
"Write your claim number on whatever wall is still standing," I told him. "Big
enough for somebody to see it."
There was a pause.
"You serious?"
"Yes," I said. "If you've got one wall left, make it useful."
And it worked.

That's the strange thing about a catastrophe. Sometimes the system functions because someone inside it stops pretending normal procedures still apply and just starts making sense where they can.

A woman called later and said, "I have a refrigerator in my living room."

I stared at my form, trying to find a box for that.

Refrigerator: displaced.

Living room: now a storage unit.

"A refrigerator," she repeated, like she needed me to understand this was not a metaphor.

"Not mine. Someone else's. It came through the wall."

She didn't cry.

She laughed once, short and sharp and not remotely amused.

"I know you can't fix that," she said. "I just needed someone to know."

That was Andrew.

People offering facts that sounded like jokes because reality had stopped checking itself for plausibility.

We typed notes into Charlie with our little codes and abbreviations, as if the right combination of

letters could translate grief into an outcome.

And every time the cursor blinked, it felt like it was asking a question no one could answer.

Now what?

There was one caller I will never forget.

His name, somehow and unbelievably, was Jose Cuervo.

He had horses.

A ranch.

Outbuildings.

Stables.

A whole life built on land and routine.

I took his call a day or two after the storm.

His voice sounded close to the receiver, like he had

been running, searching, dragging himself from one awful place to the next before finally trying a stranger in Tampa.

You could hear him walking as he talked.

Gravel.

Metal.

Something scraping.

"The water came up fast," he said.

Behind him was the after-noise of weather: loose metal, boards shifting, something
still moving
that shouldn't have been moving anymore.

"The wind took everything that could be taken.

My fences are gone."

He paused.

Swallowed.

Tried to keep his voice steady.

"My land don't look like land anymore."

And then the part he couldn't hold together.

"My horses," he said.

The word caught heavy.

"My horses are gone."

I stared at Charlie's blinking cursor like it had answers.

 Like a computer could tell me what to do
with the disappearance of living things.

 Like XXAL had a code for gone.

Gone is such a clean word for something that is not clean at all.

He called again the next day.

And the next.

Each time his voice was quieter. Thinner.

 Like fear had started to hollow him out from the
inside.

He cried on the phone with me,
 a grown man trying to say the word *horses* without
breaking apart.

He kept repeating himself.

The water.

The wind.

The noise.

As if listing it enough times might make it make sense.

It didn't.

I sat there with my headset on, staring at the same coffee ring on the laminate

desk, my pen

hovering over a form I didn't know how to fill out.

We had boxes for fences.

For barns.

For tack.

For property lines.

What box do you check for gone?

That is when you start learning what the work can take from you.

Lunch Breaks

Ruthie and I escaped in small ways, the kind you could fit into a lunch break.

We strapped on roller blades and hit the parking garage.

Concrete. Echo. Air warmer than the office. Wheels turning into a steady

rhythm that belonged

to us.

We skated in circles and laughed too loudly on purpose, letting motion shake

loose whatever the

calls had lodged in our chests.

We didn't talk about the calls out there.

We talked about nothing.

Hair. Food. A movie. Somebody's boyfriend.

Normal things.

Like we were normal women on a normal lunch break instead of refugees

from our own nervous

systems.

Then lunch ended, and we went back upstairs to our desks and headsets like we hadn't just been trying to outrun grief on eight wheels.

Management either out of decency or desperation fed us constantly.

Pizza. Cuban sandwiches. Whatever they could get.

So much pizza.

More pizza than any emotionally stable person should ever have to look at again.

We ate because the food was there and because not eating would have required a level of

principle nobody had energy for. But we kept circling the same awful thought:

How do you get a pizza delivered to a destroyed neighborhood?

To where?

To whom?

What address do you use when the address is gone?

We were not successful.

And we tried not to feel guilty chewing pepperoni while people on the other end of the line were

trying to figure out which wall still counted as their house.

After a while, the calls did two opposite things at once.

They made you deeply grateful for what you had: your roof, your faucet, your bed, your stupid

intact little routines.

And at the same time, they numbed you out.

Not because you cared less.

Because your body can't stay fully shocked for that long and still function.

Eventually, your nervous system starts rationing.

Then the phone rings again, and you remember:

This isn't a dream.

Oxygen

Then there was the mother.

Her young son was on oxygen.

This wasn't even my call, not really, but I remember it as clearly as if it were. She didn't cry the

way Jose Cuervo cried. She was too focused for that. Too scared.

Her voice had the razor-edged steadiness of someone who knows panic wastes air.

"He can't breathe without the machine," she said. "We have no power. We can't get out."

Somewhere inside the layers of chaos, broken systems, impossible logistics, jammed phone

lines, exhausted people, something started moving.

Calls went out.

Names got written down.

A chain formed in the middle of the confusion.

I don't remember who made the first call or how many hands it passed through.

I remember the moment it worked.

A helicopter.

A generator.

A child who could breathe.

When word came through that it had gotten there, applause erupted in the office.

Not polite applause.

Raw, relieved, almost furious applause, like we were trying to clap the universe back into alignment.

For one moment, the fluorescent buzz sounded softer.

Then the phones rang again.

Agent at the End of the World

Later in the day, you could usually catch me in the parking garage again on what I called a recreational smoke break.
Recreational the way drowning is recreational.
It wasn't recreation.
It was a pressure valve.
I'd lean against a concrete pillar and pull smoke into my lungs
 like I could trade it for calm.
The garage smelled like exhaust and heat and old oil, and for a few minutes the voices were distant,
muffled through walls, like the building itself was trying to hold the weight.
Whatever it took to get through the calls.
The crying.
The anxiety.
The next ring.
Then one call carved itself into me.
It was from a MetLife insurance agent in Homestead.
His voice was shaking when he started talking, the way voices do when fear has decided it's in
charge. He didn't ease into it. He dumped it all at once, like he was trying to get it out before
something happened.
"Nothing is working," he said. "No ATMs. No banks. No grocery stores. No gas."
He kept going, faster now.
"No streetlights. No signs. No electricity."
He said it didn't even matter if they wrote checks to the hurricane survivors.
There was nowhere
to cash them. It didn't even matter if you had money.
Money was just paper in a place that had slipped off the map.
"There are no vehicles to leave," he said. "There is no way out."
As he spoke, I could hear something behind him.

At first, it sounded like wind.

Then I realized it was people.

Close.

Too close.

The restless shift of feet. A voice shouting something I couldn't make out.

Then his voice changed.

It rose, sharp and sudden, the way it does when fear stops being a feeling and becomes a fact. "Send help," he yelled. "They're rocking my trailer. They're going to tip me over. Send help." In the office; everything around me kept moving. papers, pens, ringing phones,

Charlie's blinking cursor... but my body went still.

Those were the last words I ever heard from that man.

That is the moment a storm stops being weather.

It becomes aftermath.

Survival isn't only about what the wind takes.

It is about what happens next, when the phones keep ringing and the world expects you to be

normal again.

That year for Halloween, I dressed as Office Trauma, a yellow Post-it note, I dressed as the thing that haunting all of us It said: ***SEE XXAL***

Other people dressed as monsters.

---⚭---

After Andrew

At night, when I finally took the headset off, my ears still rang like the phones
had moved in and claimed squatters' rights.
I'd walk out into the parking lot, and Snoopy would be there.
Still smiling into the dark.
I'd sit in my car with the air conditioner blasting, because Florida does not care
what kind of day
you've had. The steering wheel felt slick under my hands, like I had been
holding on too hard.
Sometimes my jaw was clenched so tight my teeth hurt. Sometimes my
shoulders felt welded to
my neck.
And the strangest part was how normal everything looked outside the building.
Streetlights.
Traffic.
People at stoplights eating fries like the world had not just changed shape.
At home, I would stand in the shower longer than necessary, because water that
comes out of a
faucet on command is a luxury you don't appreciate until you spend all day
talking to people
who don't have it.
I'd wash my hair.
Wash my face.
Wash the day off.
Then I'd lie down, close my eyes, and the sound would come back anyway.
The fluorescent hum.
The phones.
The pleading.
The silence after someone says something that has no answer.
Sometimes I dreamed of Charlie's cursor blinking in the dark.

———∞———

Sometimes I woke up with my heart racing for no reason I couldn't explain to anyone who

hadn't been in that room.

People talk about disasters like they are only about what gets destroyed.

I remember that, yes.

But I also remember what gets revealed.

The man who lost everything that ran on four legs.

The child who lived because strangers refused to let the system fail him.

Both are true.

Both live with me.

And because they lived with me, Homestead kept pulling long after the phones stopped ringing.

Years later, I went.

Not right after.

Years after, when the headlines were old and the urgency had moved on to other places.

That is when it settled into my bones.

The trees were still bent, all leaning the same direction, like the wind had signed its name and

walked away. Homes were gutted. Businesses still hadn't come back. Whole blocks looked

paused mid-sentence.

Andrew wasn't there anymore.

It was quieter than that.

That is when I understood something simple and permanent:

Hurricanes don't negotiate.

They don't return what they borrow.

They don't care how long you've lived somewhere or how hard you worked for what you had.

They train you by forcing decisions sometimes loud ones, sometimes quiet ones you don't

recognize until years later, when you realize your whole life has been arranged around them.

Some storms don't need names to be remembered.

Andrew does.

And the next spring, in March of 1993, weather came for my family in a different way.

Chapter 8

The Wrong Side of Weather

Cindy loved my boys most when the house went quiet.

Not because she didn't love them loud she did but cancer had already started shrinking her world

down to what her body would allow. She tried to roughhouse sometimes. I could see her wanting

to be the aunt who chased them through the living room and let them tackle her onto the carpet.

Her body wasn't taking suggestions.

So she did what she could do.

She sat with them.

She opened a book.

She read.

The boys would lean into her, one on each side, and Cindy's voice would soften in that way it

did when she was giving her strength away on purpose.

For a little while, the room would feel normal.

Like a family.

Like time wasn't counting.

Then time did what it does.

Cindy was my older sister. We never really got along, not in the way sisters are supposed to in

movies. She was sharp where I was soft, stubborn where I was flexible. But cancer changes the

shape of everything.

She never married.

Never had children.

She dreamed of living in Florida, so she did. And for the last stretch of her life, she lived with

my family.

She loved the beach. The sand, the shore, the way the water made the world feel bigger and simpler at the same time. She could sit and watch the waves like they were telling her something important.

But by March of 1993, Cindy didn't want sun or salt air or one more round of pretending.

She wanted home.

Not Florida home.

Ohio home.

The rooms that knew her. The place where her life began, so it could be the place where it ended.

Cindy and a friend left early Friday morning, March 12.

I begged her not to go.

"A storm is coming," I said, like weather was the kind of thing you could negotiate with if you

sounded convincing enough.

Cindy listened the way she always had with that stubborn calm that made you feel both loved

and ignored.

The point wasn't the weather.

The point was Cindy.

So they went.

That same day, a cyclonic storm formed over the Gulf of Mexico, a nor'easter with ambition.

They called it the Storm of the Century, which sounds dramatic until you realize the name is

mostly a warning label.

It didn't pick a coast and behave.

It didn't stay in its lane.

It came straight through the middle of the country like it had a schedule and no patience.

All I knew was this:

My sister and the friend trying to get her home were driving straight toward it.

They barely made it to Tennessee that night.

That was the last phone call, the last real conversation before everything went quiet for good. I wish I could remember the town. What I remember is the sound: wind pushing at the line, the brittle hush underneath her words, like the storm was already inside the room with her.

Cindy's voice was softer than usual.

Careful, almost.

Like she was trying to take care of me from a hotel room.

She kept saying everything would be all right.

But I could hear the kind of snow that doesn't decorate anything.

It erases.

They couldn't get back onto I-75. Roads closed faster than they could decide.

The storm stole

exits one by one, took options away, turned the map into a lie.

They finally found a hotel.

One vacant room.

One vending machine.

Cindy's friend called me with a voice so calm it made my stomach drop.

"We found a room," she said. "We have snacks."

Snacks, in this case, meant the vending machine.

They emptied it.

Crackers.

M&M's.

Whatever would fall into the tray, they took.

And then they waited.

Three days of ice-cold white hell.

That is the only honest way to say it.

Not a "system."

Not an "event."

Just cold and wind and closures and the sickening realization that the world can decide you are

not going anywhere, no matter what you need.

At home in Florida, I did what you do when there is nothing you can do.

I turned waiting into work.

I sat by the phone like it was life support. I watched the radar. I paced the tile while the TV

stayed on low, meteorologists using that calm voice they use when they know people are scared

and don't want to make it worse.

I had lived through storms. I knew the drill.

Stock up.

Hunker down.

Make grilled cheese.

Pretend the wind isn't trying to rewrite your plans.

But this wasn't my storm.

This was my sister.

Andrew had taught me how systems move inside disaster, how help can sometimes be arranged

in the middle of ruin if enough people push in the same direction.

But with Cindy stuck in Tennessee, there was no chain to build.

No lever to pull.

No route around it.

Just weather.

Distance.

And a sister I couldn't reach.

The cruelest part was the memory my mind kept finding: Cindy beside me during the blizzard

years earlier, a blanket over both of us, the lights flickering once, her hand squeezing mine as if

to say, "I'm here."

Back then, the storm was outside the house.

And she was right there.

Now the weather had her.

And I was on the wrong side of it, empty-handed.

That kind of helplessness is its own disaster. It turns your mind into a loop. It makes you bargain

with the universe like you're customer service for grief.

If they get out of Tennessee, I'll stop worrying about the small stuff.

If they get back on I-75, I'll be grateful forever.

If she makes it home, I'll...

You don't even know what you'll do.

You'll do anything.

Sometime Monday, they made it to Ohio.

Cindy made it home.

To Mom and Dad's.

To the house that knew her.

I imagine the moment like a scene I wasn't there to witness: the car pulling in, the quiet

scramble, relief that wasn't really relief so much as exhaustion. Cindy's face tired, determined,

finally seeing the driveway that recognized her.

Ten days later, she passed away peacefully in her childhood bedroom.

The storm moved on, the way storms do.

But it left a mark anyway right across the calendar, right across my body so that even now, when

March comes around and the air goes sharp, I remember Tennessee and a hotel room and a

vending machine emptied into a tray.

Not because it's dramatic.

Because it's true.

From the outside, the years after looked ordinary: boys growing, work schedules, dinners, the daily business of keeping a family moving.

But inside me, something had shifted.

Weather had become a clock.

It marked before and after.

It marked distance.

It marked the helpless stretch between loving someone and being able to reach them.

And the next time Florida decided to speed up the clock, it wouldn't be with snow.

Itwould be with names.

Chapter 9

The Big Breakfast Queen

The years between 1993 and 2004 looked ordinary from the outside: raising boys, building routines, working, paying bills, and pretending storms were just a season not a lifestyle.

Then 2004 showed up, and Florida decided weather was now a full-time job with mandatory overtime.

That season, the names kept coming: Charley, Ivan, Jeanne.

By the time they were done,

Florida felt less like a state and more like a stress test.

Charley came first.

August.

Fast, mean, and full of the kind of confidence only a hurricane can have.

He killed people, shredded towns, and left a price tag so big it stopped sounding like money.

But only one part of that storm mattered to me.

Brenda.

My best friend.

My sister-in-law.

My person.

And if I'm honest, the reason Florida ever started feeling like home.

When Kevin and I were newlyweds, we moved south to be near her. That's the version people

like to make sound romantic: new marriage, new state, fresh start. And it was. But it was also

practical in the way real love usually is.

Brenda was family in the way that matters.

The person you can call without rehearsing.

The person who shows up.

The person who makes ordinary days feel less sharp around the edges.

She taught me a lot about life and marriage, mostly by refusing to sugarcoat either one.

But if we're being specific, the biggest thing Brenda taught me was how to cook.

I did not come from a house where food was treated like an art form. We ate. We survived.

Nobody "crafted a meal." Food was food. If it was hot and nobody cried, we called it dinner.

Brenda, on the other hand, treated the kitchen like a sanctuary and a stage. Her counters were

clean, her knives were sharp, and she had opinions about everything from onions to men.

If you walked into her kitchen, you were going to learn something whether you asked or not.

The first time I tried to help, I reached for the salt, and she snatched it away like I had grabbed a

live wire.

"Oh honey," she said, shaking her head. "Not that salt."

Then she pulled out coarse salt: big crystals, the kind that looked like they had been mined by

people who lift weights.

"This is cooking salt," she said. "That other one is desperation salt."

I laughed, because of course I did.

She did not.

Brenda cooked like she was trying to keep the world in order: heat, butter, timing, patience.

She could take leftovers and make them taste like you had planned your whole life.

"Don't crowd the pan," she would tell me. "Let it speak."

Like the ground beef had opinions.

She taught me you don't chop onions like you're mad at them. You chop onions like you're

paying attention.

She taught me garlic goes in with your whole heart.

And most of all, she taught me that feeding people is love.

Not timid love.

Not polite love.

The kind of love that says: Sit down. Eat. I'm not telling you twice.

Somewhere in those years, standing next to her stove, I became someone my family trusted with

food. Breakfast turned into cookouts. Cookouts turned into holidays. And later, after storms,

food turned into survival.

The family started calling Brenda the BBQ: Big Breakfast Queen.

It sounds like a title you win at a county fair,

but in our house it meant something.

It meant if the lights went out, she would still find a way to feed you.

Brenda loved that.

She loved any identity that came with competence and a little swagger.

By 2004, though, Brenda wasn't just teaching me to cook.

She was fighting cancer.

She lived south of us, between Punta Gorda and Fort Myers. She was already living by schedules

and medications, appointments and fatigue,

the kind of fatigue most people don't understand

unless they have watched it up close.

Cancer has its own weather system.

It changes the air in a room.

It changes what you call normal.

Brenda was brave.

But she was tired.

And then Charley started showing up on the maps.

When the spaghetti models began drawing their messy little lines toward Punta Gorda, I didn't

see a storm with a name.

I saw it headed for Brenda.

As Charley spun in the Gulf, hospitals started moving patients. On paper, it made sense: move

fragile people out of the cone, get them somewhere "safe,"

clear the path, prepare for impact.

So Brenda was transferred up the coast to St. Petersburg.

Not because anyone was careless.

Because everyone was trying to do the right thing.

And in Florida, the right thing can change every six hours.

That week is a blur of calls, updates, weather maps,

and watching the forecast like it owed me an

explanation.

I remember staring at my own hands like I could hold the storm back if I stayed

tense enough.

I had lived through hurricanes by then.

I respected weather.

I knew what it could take from a house, a street, a town.

What I didn't know, what I wasn't prepared for, was the way a storm could reach

past roofs and

windows and rearrange an illness.

How one logical decision, made in the name of safety, could become the hinge

your life swings

on.

Charley didn't give Brenda cancer.

But Charley is when the cancer stopped being something

we managed and became something

that managed us.

They took her to St. Anthony's Hospital in St. Petersburg, tucked safely inside

Tampa Bay at

least that was the idea.

A real hospital.

Doctors.

Nurses.

Generators.

Concrete.

Safe.

That was the word everyone wanted to believe in.

And plans are adorable in hurricane season.

Charley made landfall on August 13, 2004, and Florida did what Florida does: boarded up,

stocked up, waited, prayed, and pretended the waiting was a plan.

The storm itself was fast, one of those storms that doesn't linger. It hits and runs.

Later, people

called it unpredictable because it didn't come in where they thought it would.

But what mattered to me wasn't the track.

It was the shift.

The moment a hurricane stopped being something outside, something you watched on a screen

and became something inside your life, rearranging your family's reality while you stood there

holding your breath.

I wish I could tell you there was one dramatic moment when I knew everything was changing.

There wasn't.

It was smaller than that.

The way the phone rang and my stomach dropped before I even answered.

The way I started listening for bad news in every silence.

The way safe began to sound like a word people use when they don't have anything better to

offer.

After Charley, Florida didn't get to rest.

Storms don't coordinate with grief.

They don't wait their turn.

They come when they come.

Charley was the first turn of the key, the moment the door opened and the rest of that season

walked in.

And the next name on the list was Ivan.

Chapter 10
The Constant State of Almost

We were still in Tampa, still moving like people who had been holding their breath too long. Charley had barely cleared the headlines when the next forecast started lighting up. The state

hadn't even finished sweeping up. We were still checking on people, still trying to understand

how "safe" had failed Brenda, still walking around with that stunned feeling like grief and

adrenaline had switched places inside our bodies.

Then Ivan showed up on September 16 like Florida hadn't learned its lesson and needed extra

homework.

Ivan was a special kind of storm.

The kind that doesn't just arrive.

It lingers.

The kind that keeps renegotiating the terms of the agreement.

He ramped up, backed off, ramped up again strong enough and long-lived enough to turn the

whole Gulf into a threat you couldn't stop watching.

Meteorologists had a lot of words for him.

Remarkable.

Extreme.

Long-lived intensity.

I had simpler words.

Four-letter words.

Ivan could not make up his mind.

And apparently, that is a hurricane personality type.

He did a kind of hurricane salsa, throwing his projected path from Tampa to Orlando to Fort

Myers, back toward the Gulf, then starting all over again like he was dancing on Florida just to

see who would flinch first.

That was the problem.

Not just the storm.

The map.

One forecast, and Tampa looked doomed.

The next, Orlando.

Then Fort Myers.

Then back again.

Half the state was playing evacuation bingo loading cars, unloading cars, then loading them

again like it was an endurance sport nobody trained for. Hotels ran out of rooms. Roads ran out

of patience. Everyone had a cooler, a pet, a stack of important papers, and that look you get when

you're trying to stay calm for the kids while your eyes scream, *I have no idea what I'm doing.*

At some point, after one more forecast shift and one more round of Are we going? Are we

staying? We decided to fill up. So we pulled into a gas station that looked like every other

Florida gas station until you got close enough to see the truth.

Every pump had a line.

Not one car deep.

Five.

Six.

Ten.

People stood outside their vehicles with that glazed look you get when you've been awake too

long and are trying to remain civilized out of spite.

A woman held a toddler on one hip and a Styrofoam cup of coffee in the other like it was the last

stable thing left in her life. A man in flip-flops argued into a cell phone so hard his neck turned

red.

Someone yelled, "They're out of ice!"

You would have thought they had announced the end of electricity.

And in a way, they had.

Because ice is how Floridians pretend we still have control. If the storm takes the power, we will simply build a cooler empire and live out of it like rugged pioneers except with deli meat and denial.

We got in line anyway.

Of course we did.

When it was finally our turn, the pump clicked off after a sad little trickle, like it was tired too.

Kevin stared at the numbers like he could intimidate them into filling the tank.

"Is that it?" I asked.

"That's it," he said.

Somewhere behind us, a car horn blared. Someone shouted something about idiots and this state

and why do we live here.

Which, honestly, was fair.

We drove away with half a tank and a full-body tension headache and went home.

By then, Ivan had turned normal life into a constant state of almost.

Almost leaving.

Almost staying.

Almost hitting us.

Almost sparing us.

Almost letting us sleep.

That is what I remember most.

Not the final numbers, though there were plenty.

Deaths.

Billions in damage.

Tornadoes flicking off his outer bands like sparks.

Surf that looked less like water and more like an argument.

I remember the waiting.

Waiting did something physical to me. The tension between my shoulders climbed through my

neck like it wanted to explode out my ears. My jaw stayed clenched. My body acted like it was

bracing for impact even when nothing had hit yet.

Charley had been brutal and fast.

A hit-and-run.

Ivan was something else.

Ivan had the energy of someone who shows up to the party uninvited, rearranges your furniture,

eats your snacks, then stands in the doorway like: *I might leave. I might not. Let's see how you*

behave.

There were moments watching the forecast shift again when I felt something that surprised me. Not just fear.

Anger.

Because fear makes sense. Fear is your body trying to keep you alive.

But Ivan felt personal.

Like being toyed with.

Like being tested.

Like being reminded the state you live in is basically a peninsula with a gambling problem.

And underneath all of it was the other thing, the thing we didn't say out loud because it was still

too tender.

Brenda.

Charley had already changed the terms of our lives. We were trying to understand what was

happening to her and still deal with hurricane season at the same time, as if grief and weather

could be carried in the same hands.

We were still trying to live in a world where "safe" had turned into a word with loose edges.

Ivan didn't care.

Storms don't glance at your calendar and say, *Oh bad timing. We'll come back later.*

They show up anyway.

After days of watching, waiting, and trying to outguess a storm with commitment issues, Ivan

finally made his choice.

He didn't hit us directly.

It should have felt like relief.

Part of it did.

But mostly, it felt thin.

Not joyful.

Not grateful in the clean, cinematic way people imagine relief is supposed to feel.

More like collapse.

More like the moment after a fire alarm stops ringing and your body still doesn't

trust the

silence.

We had spent days bracing.

Days checking maps.

Checking supplies.

Checking each other.

By the time Ivan wandered off, there wasn't much celebration left in us.

Just exhaustion.

That was the lesson:

Not every storm has to hit you head-on to leave a mark.

Sometimes almost is enough.

Sometimes the waiting does its own damage.

Ivan passed, but he left us altered anyway.

And Florida, having barely exhaled, turned toward the

next name. Jeanne.

Chapter 11
Dinner in the Dark

Jeanne wasn't nice.

She was angry, and I still don't know why.

She tore things up.

Dropped trees like punctuation. Hit Tampa and St. Petersburg hard enough
that both cities seemed to brace, hold, and flinch.

Which mattered, because St. Petersburg is where Brenda had been evacuated after
Charley.

She was at St. Anthony's Hospital, dying of cancer.

They protected patients the best they could,

but a hospital in a hurricane is still a hospital in a
hurricane.

They moved people into hallways away from windows, away from glass because
sometimes that is the safest place left.

Later, the stories filtered out: the roof bouncing, rain pouring in, patients lying
there while the
building argued with the sky.

Afterward, people put numbers to Jeanne, because numbers are how we pretend
we can hold
something like that. Thousands died across the Caribbean, most of them in Haiti.
In Florida, they
called it "only" a handful.

But grief doesn't understand statistics.

Grief doesn't compare.

Grief doesn't round down.

In our world, only one mattered.

Not long after that hurricane trio, my sister-in-law passed.

Gone to heaven.

And here's what's cruel about timing: the world doesn't pause because you're
losing someone. It
keeps asking you to manage things.

 It keeps demanding logistics. It keeps piling ordinary needs
on top of extraordinary grief,
like the universe is testing how much one family can carry without
dropping anything.

In the mornings, I either took a cold shower that required more courage than I always had, or I stopped by the YMCA and borrowed hot water like a small luxury I hadn't earned but desperately needed.

There is something humbling about standing under a communal shower after a hurricane, trying

to look normal while everyone around you does the same quiet math:

How long will this last?

How much did you lose?

Are you okay?

Nobody asked out loud.

Floridians are excellent at not asking the question that might make you cry.

Then I'd go to work and do what people do after storms: act like this is

temporary.

Like this is fine.

At night, we repeated the ritual.

Feed them.

Laugh with them.

Send them back to light.

Then settle into the humid dark again.

We suffered in the dark so they wouldn't have to.

And I'd do it again.

Every time.

One night it was burgers and corn on the cob, eaten off paper plates because dishes are for

people with electricity. Another night it was chicken overcooked because the grill didn't care

about my grief and chips passed around like side dishes.

We ate outside in the heavy air, citronella burning, neighbors' generators growling in the

distance like exhausted animals. The world was dark and sticky and altered, but the boys were

laughing at something stupid, and for ten minutes I could breathe.

Our house was still standing.

The yard was not.

Trees down.

Debris everywhere.

And we had no electricity for two and a half weeks.

I now know the dog days of summer are definitely August in Florida. August is when the

temperature is ninety-seven, the humidity is one hundred, and merely thinking too hard can make

you sweat enough to reconsider your entire life.

So we sent the boys to neighbors across town.

Not because we didn't want them with us.

Because we did.

But the neighbors had electricity. They had hot showers. Lights that turned on. Beds that didn't

feel like survival training. Over there, the morning alarm clock could still do its job and get them

to school like the world hadn't cracked open.

Every evening, the boys came home.

Every evening,

I fed them like we were still a normal family having a normal week.

We grilled. We cooked outside. We sat together and ate, because dinner was the one thing I could still make reliable.

We laughed when we could.

We pretended just for a little while that

wind hadn't rearranged our lives.

Then every night, they went back to a cool house.

A bright house.

A house with working outlets.

And Kevin and I stayed.

We lived in the dark.

We slept in the dark.

Then it was time to send them away again.

That part never got easier.

Jeanne had pulled trees out of the ground by their roots

and laid them across the road.

For a few days, no cars were getting in or out of our neighborhood,

which would have been fine except we

still needed ice because I was determined to keep feeding everybody

like nothing had changed.

So I did what made sense in a heat-induced lapse of judgment.

I got on my bicycle and headed for Publix.

It was Florida hot.

The kind of heat that doesn't sit on you.

It claims you.

The humidity hit like a hot, wet towel.

 I was sweating in places I didn't know could sweat.

I pedaled harder because the sun was judging me,

and the ice was calling my name.

By the time I got there,

 I looked like I had lost a very personal argument with the weather.

I grabbed the ice.

I grabbed wine, because morale is a strategy.

And when I walked up to the register,

I realized the cashier lived around the corner from me.

She didn't have electricity either. I don't even know if she had a car.

She looked at me.

Looked at the ice.

Then said, "Guess we're all improvising these days."

We smiled the kind of smile you only have

when you are tired in the exact same way.

Right there, over melting ice and a very

necessary bottle of wine, we recognized each other.

That was bonding.

Trauma bonding, probably.

It sets in early.

I rode home with the ice sloshing and the wine clinking like fragile hope, pedaling faster and then faster than that, because nothing motivates cardio like the sound of your dinner plan turning into soup.

That night, we grilled whatever had thawed the most.

Fish.

Chicken.

Mystery meat with potential.

The boys filled their bellies.

I filled my wine glass.

We laughed.

What I remember most isn't a particular meal.

It's the deck.

It's the Alafia River sitting there like it hadn't done anything wrong quiet, brown, rising and falling with the tide.
The Alafia River never came for the house the way the wind came for the trees.

But it rose enough to make a play for our boat.

The boat was new to us: a blue-and-white twenty-foot Sea Pro meant to satisfy every member of the family. Fishing for Kevin and Kris. Tubing for Kyle. Wakeboarding for Kevin Jr. Sun and water skiing for me. All of us pretending compromise was a kind of recreation.

We loved that boat in the hopeful way you love something you haven't owned long enough to resent yet.
It felt like weekends.

It felt like fun.

It felt like proof we were still allowed to plan for something good.

Then the river rose, and that beautiful blue boat sat wrong in the water: low, tilted, taking on more of the Alafia than a boat should ever have to hold.

That's when Leroy showed up.

Handlebar mustache first.

Grin from ear to ear.

Leroy was our nextdoor neighbor, and he had the kind of face that always looked like it had seen

a problem before and wasn't especially impressed by this one. He came over to help Kevin save

our sinking boat from the rising waters of the Alafia River, because that is what people do here:

they see trouble, and they walk toward it.

The two of them wrestled ropes and weight and water while I stood on land offering

encouragement that was mostly useless but deeply heartfelt.

It was one more ridiculous scene in an already ridiculous season.

My sister-in-law dying.

The power out.

Trees down everywhere.

The boys sleeping somewhere else.

And now our new family boat trying to become part of the river.

But they saved it.

Or maybe they just refused to let it go, which isn't exactly the same thing but in Florida, it counts

for plenty.

And that more than any one meal is what I remember about those weeks.

Not just the darkness.

Not just the grilling.

Not just the boys laughing over silly dinner jokes while the world felt broken around the edges.

I remember the river.

I remember Leroy.

I remember my husband refusing to surrender one more thing.

For those evenings, the storm wasn't the whole story.

We were still a family.

After 2004, I thought I understood Florida storms.

I thought I understood what it meant to lose power, lose trees, lose sleep, lose

someone you love

and still get dinner on the table.

Then the years passed.

Quiet on the outside.

Busy on the inside.

Storms came and went. The boys grew. Life refilled the house.

And I didn't know yet that one day the storm wouldn't just test the house.

It would test the whole map of my life.

Chapter 12

The Storms Without Names
In the years after Jeanne, life did what life always does: it kept moving, even
when I wanted it to hold still long enough for me to catch up.

Brenda was gone. The storms were gone. The power came back. The trees
were cut and dragged and chipped into neat piles, as if neat piles could count
as closure. The boys came home. Kevin went back to work.

And I went back to doing what women do when a family gets hit by grief and
weather in the
same season.

I kept the day moving.

Which is not the same thing as healing, but from the outside, it can look close
enough.
The years after weren't dramatic in any movie way. Nobody stood in a
doorway with a
meaningful cup of coffee and a lesson learned. We just lived. We replaced what
needed
replacing. We cleaned what could be cleaned. We made dinners. We paid bills.
The house filled back in.

We built routines the ordinary ones that don't feel sacred until they're gone.

Saturday mornings, I'd get up early, before anybody else, and do the grocery
run while the house was still asleep. Two hours and four hundred dollars later,
I'd come home with the trunk full and the day already loud. By then,
everybody was awake and unloading bags like a pit crew that ran
on cereal and sarcasm.

It was never peaceful exactly.

But it was ours.

And no matter what else happened, we ate dinner together every night. That
part mattered to me. The whole family at the table every single night and
everybody had to answer the same two questions:

What was the best thing that happened to you today?

And what was the worst?

Some nights the answers were funny. Some nights they were dumb. Some nights somebody tried to get away with "nothing," and I wouldn't let them.
Not because I wanted a confession.
Because I wanted connection.
I wanted proof we still belonged to each other.
That's what people forget when they talk about "the big events." Most of family life isn't big.
It's groceries and homework and dishes and hearing three versions of the same story from three
boys who all think they're the funniest person in the room.
It's repetition.
Which is another way of saying love, if you do it long enough.
Hurricane season became part of the calendar the way Lent is for Catholics or football is for
people with emotional stamina. Every year, you watched. Every year, you stocked batteries and
water. Every year, you told yourself maybe this one would slide somewhere else.
You learned storm names before you needed them, which is a strange way to live if you stop and
think about it for more than five seconds.
And while I kept one eye on the sky, the boys grew up.
That sentence is too small for what it means.
They didn't just get taller. They got opinions. They got car keys. They got girlfriends. They got
the kind of confidence that is beautiful in your own children and alarming in everyone else's.
They became people who could leave the house under their own power and make decisions I
wasn't there to supervise.
Which, to be clear, is the goal of parenting.
And also its cruelest joke.
Kris was my first everything: first child, first to walk, first to skateboard, first to waterski, first to
ride out a hurricane, first to get married, first to have children of his own.
First and so far only to get in trouble with the law, because apparently even his milestones liked
variety.

When the boys were little, all three of them were escorted from elementary school across the

street to the park, where I picked them up after work. One day, Kris wasn't there.

The other two had crossed.

He had not.

No one had seen him.

The sheriff eventually found him at the Eckerd drugstore, where he had attempted to steal a cigar

and a lighter.

My boy went to juvie.

Not exactly a scrapbook moment, but there we were.

Kris has always had a way of making life interesting. Sometimes wonderful-interesting.

Sometimes call-your-mother-and-sit-down-interesting. But he was my first, and first children

have a way of training you before you know you are the one being trained.

Kyle was my comic relief.

He got that honestly from me.

He could ride a skateboard like he had signed a private agreement with gravity fearless on

pavement, all charm with adults, and dangerously smooth with the ladies.

But put that boy near open water and one suspicious-looking cloud, and suddenly he became

everybody's emergency manager, lobbying to get the boat out immediately and preferably

yesterday.

Once, we got Kyle to sit on a surfboard and let us tow him. He panicked and screamed that a

shark was following him.

It was the leash to the surfboard.

In his defense, fear is not always detail-oriented.

Kevin Jr. will always be my baby, but when I had nothing left in me, he became my rock. He

learned loyalty and hard work from his dad, which he may or may not admit.

By the age of three, Kevin Jr. could use a tape measure. Granted, everything measured the same:

813-932-6002.

Our home phone number.

But still.

It was a start.

Raising three boys with Kevin was its own adventure, loud, funny, exhausting, rarely still, and

never a dull moment. Kevin and I became professionals at playing good cop, bad cop, depending

on which boy was pushing back and how committed that particular son felt to testing us that day.

Kevin was a granite guy steady and hard and he taught them how to work.

How to keep going.

How to take responsibility seriously.

That kind of fathering leaves a mark.

Mostly, it was a good one.

Then one day, the rooms got quieter.

Somewhere in all that motion the parenting, the managing, the smoothing over, the staying one

step ahead of whatever came next I misplaced something of my own.

Not all at once.

Not in a noble way.

I just kept following his lead because it was easier not to make waves. Easier to keep the family

together than to stop and ask where I had gone inside it.

Because that's what wives and mothers did.

At least, that was the way I had been trained.

Then the boys grew up and left, and the center of our universe moved out.

What remained wasn't just silence.

It was a question:

If I'm no longer needed in all the old ways, who exactly am I?

Nobody prepares you for how surreal an empty nest feels. You spend years begging for five

minutes alone, and then suddenly the house hands you all of it at once.

The silence doesn't feel peaceful at first.

It feels suspicious.

You walk past a clean bedroom and think something must be wrong. You stop buying certain

snacks. You stop cooking with the same urgency because nobody is going to burst through the

door starving at 4:20 p.m. like a small, sweaty tornado with homework.

And when that rhythm changes, your marriage changes too.

Not always dramatically.

Sometimes quietly the way weather changes before people admit it.

Drifting from your spouse can feel a lot like missing the signs of a hurricane.

The pressure shifts.

The light changes. The air feels different. And by the time you say, *Something's off,* the outer

bands are already here.

But unlike a storm, a marriage can be steered.

You can notice.

You can turn toward each other.

You can choose again.

Whether you do is the hard part.

Our house changed too not just physically, though houses always do. It changed because

memory kept moving in. After enough years, a home becomes less of a structure and more like

an archive.

Every room held a version of us.

Every hurricane season added another layer to the way we watched the sky.

And without asking my permission, I got used to living with one eye on the forecast.

Not in a dramatic way.

In a Florida way.

Casually.

Competently.

With canned goods and irony.

That may be the most dangerous kind of experience the kind that makes you think you

understand what's coming.

By the time 2017 rolled around, the boys were grown enough to scatter when weather threatened.

Old enough to have plans that didn't include asking my permission. Old enough to be building

lives I wasn't always standing close enough to witness.

That is the thing no one tells you.

Families change shape.

Storms do too.

And then one day you realize you are no longer the mother in the doorway calling everyone

inside.

You are the mother waiting for the text that says they made it somewhere safe.

Maybe that is its own kind of faith.

Not that nothing bad will happen.

Not that you can control the weather.

Just that love can keep stretching without breaking.

By the end of 2004, I thought I understood storms better.

Charley. Ivan. Jeanne.

The names came one after another, like Florida was reading from a list and daring us to keep up.

We lost power. We lost trees. We lost sleep. We lost Brenda. We rearranged our days around

heat, batteries, food, children, and whatever patience we had left.

We learned how quickly ordinary life could become primitive.

But what I did not understand yet was that not every storm announces itself on radar.

Some storms do not come with names.

Some do not make landfall all at once.

Some move into your life quietly and begin rearranging things from the inside.

Between Jeanne and Irma, there were years of my life that did not belong to weather at all.

Between 2004 and 2017, I lived through drug abuse, shame, recovery, and the long, humiliating work of becoming someone I could trust again.

I will not dress that up.

I will not make it neat.

And I will not hand it more pages than it gets to own.

But if this story is going to tell the truth about survival, then it has to tell this truth too:

By the time the Gulf came for my home, I already knew what it meant to lose yourself and fight

your way back.

That, more than anything, is what carried me from Jeanne to Irma.

Some came with names.

Some didn't.

Chapter 13

When the Forecast Gets Loud

Irma came in like a whirlwind, which, at this point, felt less like weather and more like a

personal theme.

I was not prepared.

The night before Irma, I was at happy hour with coworkers, celebrating somebody's something:

a birthday, an anniversary, a victory over paperwork. It doesn't matter now. What matters is that

I was out raising a glass while Kevin was at home battening down the hatches and silently composing my eulogy.

When I walked in, he gave me that look.

The one that says:

I love you .

But also,if this house blows away,I'm telling theinsurance   company it was your fault.

The next morning, we were supposed to leave for a Princess Cruise to Alaska. Two weeks.
Planned.
Paid for. Optimism in receipt form.
Irma, meanwhile, was doing what hurricanes do shifting, swelling, turning the entire state into a room full of people staring at maps like they were tarot cards. Everybody was suddenly an
amateur meteorologist and a professional Panicker.
The kids were safe, as far as I knew.
And "kids" is generous. Kris was married and living in California, building his own family. Happy, healthy, and loving
life.
Kyle was married too, living in New York because he was going to be a star very soon. Happy, hungry, and loving life.

Kevin Jr. was still in Florida, living a block away. He was grown, technically, which meant he

was old enough to make his own decisions and young enough to make them with the timing of a hurricane.

He and his girlfriend, Cady, "evacuated" to Pennsylvania.

I put evacuated in quotes because it was also, conveniently, an opportunity to visit Cady's mother.

 Which is how Florida works. A hurricane shows up, and suddenly everyone is making choices that would have sounded unhinged in a calm week.

Sure, we'll drive across several states.

Sure, we'll turn it into a family visit.

Sure, we'll just see what happens.

Hurricanes don't just move through your zip code. They rearrange your calendar. They make

normal feel optional, and life goes right on happening anyway because life has never been polite.

At Tampa International, our flight was delayed because of course it was, and the airport turned

into a live-action group therapy session. Suitcases everywhere. Weather apps refreshed like

rosary beads. Everyone talking too brightly, like if they joked hard enough, the storm might take he hint.

I kept checking my phone, doing that maternal math you do when you can't physically see your children.

Where are they?

Do they have gas?

Is their plan an actual plan, or just optimism wearing a name tag?

Kevin Jr. texted that they were fine.

Made it to Pennsylvania, he said like Pennsylvania was a magical word that meant immune.

My worry shifted to Oliver.

Oliver is a cockatoo, which means he doesn't just observe the world.

He announces it.

Loudly.

With authority.

This is the same bird who would sit on his perch in the front yard and, if a seagull or anything

with wings flew overhead, he would scream:

"EAGLE! OLIVER! CAGE! RIGHT NOW!"

And of course, we'd immediately take Oliver to his cage, because apparently Oliver was both the

early warning system and the emergency broadcast service.

So when Kevin put him in a sanctuary before we left, I understood.

Oliver knew this wasn't good.

He had been watching the sky like it owed him money. I could practically hear him narrating it

in his furious little voice:

BAD WEATHER.

BAD DECISION.

YOUR FAULT.

The house? Negotiable.

The fence? Negotiable.

The yard? Negotiable.

The bird?

The bird had to be okay.

So we left town for two weeks come hell, high water, or Hurricane Irma because this trip was

happening whether Florida approved or not. For once, I wasn't chasing a spaghetti model.

This was planned.

Prepaid.

Virtuous.

And Alaska did what Alaska does.

Showed off.

We were kayaking near glaciers, black water, blue ice, air so cold it felt clean
and I was still thinking about roof shingles.

On the ship, they made those calm announcements:
Good morning, guests… please enjoy the show.

And my brain translated automatically:
Secure loose items.
Evacuate now.
Find a safe place.
I smiled at the buffet and nodded at strangers like I was present, but inside, I was
back home, picturing the yard turning into airborne debris and the roof lifting off
our life in my imagination panels peeling up like pages, everything we owned
suddenly light enough to leave.
I was surrounded by wonder.
And I was still counting what could be taken.
Halfway through the trip, my phone buzzed.
A text from Kevin Jr.
There was a picture attached Kevin Jr. and Cady, dressed up, smiling so hard it
looked like it
hurt. The kind of smile you wear when you have just done something huge and
are still half-
waiting for the universe to object.
The message read:
Look what we did today.
That was it.
No warning.
No soft opening.
No *Mom, don't freak out.*
Just a photo, one sentence, and an instant before-and-after.

They had gotten married.

In Pennsylvania.

While Florida was bracing for Irma and I was floating past glaciers
pretending not to think about plywood.

Two feelings hit at the same time.

I was happy.

Genuinely happy.

Because it was them.

Because it was good.

Because in a life that had taught me what storms can take, here was
something being made
instead.

And I was angry.

Not at them.

Not really.

I was angry because I wanted to be there.

I wanted to see it with my own eyes instead of through a screen. I wanted to
hug my son, fix
Cady's hair, cry like mothers do, complain about the lack of notice while
taking seventeen
pictures and insisting I didn't look my age.

I wanted the moment.

But hurricanes don't ask what you want.

They scatter people across states and schedules and airports and cruise ships.

Later, after the first sting wore off, I could see the strange grace in it.

Irma hadn't destroyed this.

She had accidentally made room for it.

Kevin Jr. and Cady had gone to Pennsylvania for safety or, more honestly, safety plus a visit to Cady's mother and in the middle of all that weather chaos, they made a decision that was steady.

A mother-in-law can be a lot like a hurricane, I realized.

Not because she's destructive.

Because she can change the trajectory of your life with one firm push and a smile that says, *This isforthebest.*

And sometimes, she's right.

We came back to Florida, and it wasn't nearly as bad as it could have been.

There was damage.

There always is.

But it wasn't devastation. Not the life-rearranging kind. Not the kind that replaces your

vocabulary with one word:

Gone.

Still, standing there afterward, I had the strangest feeling.

Not relief.

Recognition.

It was starting to feel like hurricanes weren't just things I lived through.

When the forecast gets loud, everybody makes decisions.

Irma didn't take the house.

She did take the dock.

Yes, that was apparently all my fault.

But in the middle of all that rearranging, she also added to the family.

A daughter-in-law.

A new branch.

A story we would tell for years, because every family needs at least one wedding announcement delivered by text message during a hurricane while the mother of the groom is somewhere near a glacier pretending to be calm.

That was Irma's lesson.

Sometimes a storm doesn't just scatter people.

Sometimes it shows you where they are going.

And not long after that, I made a decision of my own.

Chapter 14

A Room That Belonged to Me

Shortly after Irma, something changed in me.

Not all at once. Not like a movie where the woman looks in the mirror, squares her shoulders,

and becomes somebody new by the next scene. It was quieter than that.

More inconvenient.

Like a hairline crack you don't notice until the light hits it just right and then one day you realize

the whole thing has been split for a while.

We had been married for thirty-five years.

That's long enough to have a whole language made of shortcuts. Long enough to communicate

with sighs and glances. Long enough to know where the other person will stand in the kitchen

without looking. Long enough to forget where you end and the marriage begins.

And still, something in me shifted.

Not anger, exactly.

Not hatred.

Not even the kind of heartbreak people understand quickly.

It felt more like clarity.

Like waking in the middle of the night and realizing the sound you've been hearing for years

isn't the house settling.

It's something else.

Irma wasn't the worst storm I had lived through not by a long shot. But it did what storms

sometimes do: it put a bright light on what was already true.

There is something about preparing for a hurricane that strips life down to its bones. You board

up. You move things. You make piles. You decide what matters and what can be lost.

You tell yourself you are organizing a house, when really life is asking a much ruder question:

What are you still trying to save?
Somewhere in all that ordinary hurricane ritual, something in me went still.
Not the angry kind of still.
The clear kind.
Because it wasn't just about the storm. It was about how often I had
swallowed my own knowing
to keep things calm. How often I had made myself smaller so the weather
inside the house
wouldn't change.
I remember thinking, with sudden, quiet certainty:
I do not want to live like this anymore.
So I left.
I don't say that lightly, because nothing about leaving a life you built is light.
Thirty-five years
has weight. Thirty-five years has paperwork. Thirty-five years has
photographs in boxes and
habits in your hands and a thousand tiny agreements you didn't know you
had made until you try
to break them.
We separated, and I did something that, for most of my life, would have
sounded like a sentence
from somebody else's story.
I went to live alone.
Treasure Island, Florida.
A strip of sand and sky and saltwater stubbornness. A place where the Gulf
looks innocent until
it doesn't. A place people visit for sunsets and vacations and the illusion that
everything can be
rinsed clean.
That first key to my own place felt heavier than it should have. It was just
metal, nothing fancy,
but it opened a door nobody else expected me to manage alone.
For the first time in a long time, I could lock a door behind me and know
the quiet on the other
side belonged to me.
I didn't go there to be dramatic.

I went because I needed a room that belonged to me. A quiet that didn't require permission. A set of decisions that were mine from start to finish, what to eat, when to sleep, how loud the TV should be, whether the house should be warm or cold or lit up like a lighthouse.

I didn't know how to live alone.

Not really.

By then, I had spent so many years being part of a unit: wife, mother, manager of moods and

meals and logistics that solitude felt less like freedom and more like a question.

Who am I when I am not organizing my life around everyone else?

I knew how to be a wife.

I knew how to be a mother.

I knew how to keep the machine running even when parts were missing.

What I did not know was how to sit in a quiet apartment and hear my own thoughts without

flinching.

The first night, I stood in the doorway with a bag in my hand and listened.

No boys coming in and out.

No "Mom, where's ..."

No footsteps.

No familiar noises that used to irritate me and then, the minute they were gone, became proof I wasn't alone.

Just the soft hum of the refrigerator and the distant sound of waves, like a constant exhale.

The bed looked too big.

The bathroom looked almost staged.

One sink.

One toothbrush.

That may have been the loneliest thing of all.

I put my bag down and looked around like I was trespassing in my own life.
Then I did what any newly alone woman does when she doesn't know what
to do with freedom:
I ate cereal for dinner.
Not cute cereal.
Not wholesome cereal.
Just whatever was in the box.
I sat on the couch with a bowl in my lap and realized nobody was going to be
disappointed.
Nobody was going to comment. Nobody was going to ask if that was my plan
for dinner.
And then I realized I was disappointed anyway.
Because I didn't want freedom in the form of cereal.
I wanted freedom in the form of peace.
Later, I took my phone and walked down to the beach like a teenager like a
person with no one
to report back to. The water was dark, the sky wide, the air thick with salt. A
few people were
still out: couples, tourists, the kind of folks who think the ocean is always
friendly because they
have never met it angry.
I stood there barefoot in the sand and let the waves do what waves do.
Come in.
Go out.
Come in again.
Steady and reliable as breath.
And the strangest part was this:
I was both terrified and relieved.
Terrified because I had done the thing women my age aren't supposed to do.
We are supposed to
endure. We are supposed to keep the family glued together with our bare
hands. We are
supposed to shrink our needs until they fit in whatever space is left.

Relieved because, for the first time in a long time, my nervous system stopped bracing for
impact.

I'm not saying my marriage was a villain. I'm not rewriting history to make my leaving look
noble. There were good years. There was laughter. There was building and raising and all the
ordinary heroism that comes with staying.

But something had been missing for a long time, and Irma was a kind of mirror.

Not because it was the worst storm.

Because it reminded me how quickly life can change and how little time you get to keep handing
yourself away.

Time is not generous.

Time is just time.

It passes whether you are living or only existing.

After Irma, I started asking questions I had avoided because they were too sharp:

Is this my life?

Is this how I want to spend what's left of it?

If I keep choosing everyone else, will there be anything left of me to choose?

The answers didn't arrive with fireworks.

They arrived the way truth usually does:

Quiet.

Steady.

Impossible to unknow.

So there I was, on Treasure Island.

And that was the beginning of my second life.

Not a myth.

Not a reinvention.

A real life.

I learned how to carry my own groceries without making it a metaphor. I learned how to take out

the trash without resentment. I learned that silence can be lonely, yes, but it can also be holy.

I built a small, ordinary life on purpose.

I became a regular at places.

I learned people's names.

I rode my bike everywhere like I was sixteen and had nothing to lose but dignity.

Treasure Island did not give me paradise first.

It gave me room.

And after a lifetime of making room for everyone else, that felt like a miracle.

The island didn't fix me.

It gave me space to hear myself.

And once I had room, Treasure Island started teaching me what to do with it.

Chapter 15

The Island Let Me Be

Before the storms took Treasure Island from me, it gave me myself.

That sounds dramatic, but it wasn't.

It was ordinary.

Which is probably why I trusted it.

It was sunsets and bike rides and Gulf Boulevard traffic. It was walking into my American

Legion and sitting on my bar stool. It was tourists asking questions, locals pretending not to love

them, and the Gulf glittering like it had never hurt anybody in its life.

For the first time in my life, I belonged somewhere that did not need me to be useful.

Treasure Island just let me be.

By the time I had been there a while, my little life had started arranging itself around small

rituals.

Coffee.

Work.

The beach.

The bike.

Publix runs on Gulf Boulevard.

The American Legion.

Sunsets that looked fake enough to be rude.

I rode my bike everywhere, partly because it was practical and partly because it made me feel

free in a way I hadn't felt since I was young. There is something ridiculous and wonderful about

being a grown woman on a bicycle with groceries in the basket,

pretending you are both

responsible and sixteen at the same time.

Some days, I rode to Publix like I was on an important diplomatic mission.

Milk.

Bread.

Something for dinner.

Something I absolutely did not need but bought anyway because I was unsupervised.

That was one of the quiet luxuries of living alone. Nobody questioned the cart. Nobody looked at

my purchases and said, "Is that dinner?" Nobody had an opinion about whether cheese and

crackers counted as a meal.

In my house, they did.

Treasure Island made room for that version of me.

The easy version.

The woman who could stop and talk to strangers. The woman who could walk home from the

Legion and feel the salt air wrap around her shoulders. The woman who could stand at the

water's edge and not be needed by anyone for a few minutes.

That was new.

Not being needed.

At first, I didn't trust it.

Then I started to love it.

The island had its own rhythm. Mornings were bright and slow. Afternoons smelled like

sunscreen, fried food, and hot pavement. Evenings belonged to the sunset crowdtourists lined

up with phones, locals pretending we weren't also looking, and the sky showing off like it had a

contract with God.

People came to Treasure Island to feel young, rested, romantic, healed, tipsy, sunburned, or

briefly less disappointed in their lives.

I lived there.

That was different.

Living there meant learning the shortcuts and the weather moods. It meant knowing when the

beach would be packed and when it would be quiet. It meant understanding that tourists will ask

where to eat while standing thirty feet from three restaurants.

And I loved them for it.

Mostly.

There is a special kind of pride that comes from giving directions in a place that has finally

started to feel like yours.

The American Legion became part of that life for a while.

Post 158.

A place where the drinks were affordable, the stories got better after the second round, and

everybody knew just enough about everybody else to be dangerous.

I remember one exact date with absurd clarity.

March 17.

St. Patrick's Day.

A friend and I had barely started our bike ride when we decided it was a perfectly reasonable

hour to stop at the Legion for our usual two-dollar Bloody Marys, which felt less like a drink special and more like a public service.

So we did.

Then we got back on our bikes and finished our usual loop around the island the kind of ordinary routine that feels permanent while you're living it.

An hour later, maybe a little more, we came back around just in time to watch Jimmy put a sign on the door:

CLOSED DUE TO PANDEMIC.

And just like that, the world tilted.

Not with the drama of a hurricane.

No boarded windows.

No weather maps.

No lawn furniture flying into the Gulf. Just a sign on a door.

Sometimes that's all it takes.

I stood there staring at it, thinking, *Now what are we supposed to do for fun?* which was admittedly not the grandest possible response to a global crisis, but it was honest.

The loss of normal life rarely arrives looking historic.

At first, it just feels rude.

Then the island emptied.

No tourists dragging coolers.

No bars spilling laughter onto sidewalks.

No cheerful little traffic jams caused by people who had never driven near a beach before.

The roads went quiet.

The beach went wide and nearly private.

Even the light felt different.

It was eerie.

It was sad.

And if I'm being honest, it was a little bit beautiful.

For a while, Treasure Island felt like it belonged to only me.

Not in any legal sense, obviously. I didn't suddenly become queen of Gulf Boulevard, although I

would like to say I had the calves for it.

But in the deep, private way a place can belong to you when it has gone still enough for you to

hear yourself inside it.

I rode my bike down streets so empty they looked staged, like a movie set waiting for actors who

never arrived. I could hear things I had never noticed before: gulls, wind shifting through palms,

the click of my own tires on the pavement.

The emptiness of the island mirrored something I was learning to tolerate in myself:

Space.

Solitude.

The strange ache of a life stripped down to essentials.

It wasn't normal. It wasn't healthy. It is not something I would wish back.

But there was something almost sacred in the stillness.

After years of making myself small inside my own life, I was living in a place quiet

enough to

hold me exactly as I was.

That was Treasure Island too.

Not just sunsets and sea oats and salt air.

Community.

Ritual.

Familiar faces.

And then, just as quickly, absence.

Maybe that's why I loved it so much.

It didn't just give me paradise.

It gave me room.

It gave me back the woman I had misplaced somewhere between marriage,

motherhood, work,

survival, and everybody else's needs.

And it did it without making a speech.

Treasure Island was not sentimental.

It was too sandy for that.

It gave me sunsets and humidity.

Tourists and traffic.

Cheap drinks and bad parking.

Bike rides and beach walks.

Rainstorms that came in sideways and left me laughing

because apparently Florida believed noses needed rinsing from the inside.

It gave me ordinary.

And ordinary, after a certain age, is not ordinary at all.

Ordinary is proof.

Proof that you have a routine.

Proof that you have a place to go.

Proof that somebody knows your drink, your name, your bike, your laugh, your

preferred seat, or

at least your general nonsense.

By 2022, I thought I finally understood island life.

The rhythms.

The seasons.

The shortcuts.

The way storms usually behaved.

That's what comfort does.

It makes you believe you're fluent.

Years of sunsets can make you forget the Gulf keeps receipts.

I had mistaken familiarity for safety.

I had mistaken routine for permanence.

I had mistaken the island's kindness for a promise.

And then Ian showed up to correct me.

Chapter 16
Recovery Is Its Own Weather

Four years is long enough to get comfortable.

Long enough to start thinking you understand a place. Long enough to believe you've paid your

dues and earned a little peace as a resident perk.

By then, I had been living on the island for four years, watching sunsets, learning the rhythms,

and having the time of my life. Island life will hypnotize you if you let it. Salt air as therapy.

Neighbors who wave like they mean it. The Gulf glittering out there like beauty itself can be

trusted.

Even hurricane season starts to feel familiar.

Not safe.

Just manageable.

Like something you plan for the way other people plan for taxes or in-laws: grim acceptance, a

Costco run, and the hope everyone behaves.

Batteries.

Water.

Shutters.

Flashlights.

Generator debates.

The yearly ritual of staring at a cone and wondering who was going to blink first.

Then Ian showed up.

Ian made landfall near Fort Myers on September 28, 2022, as a Category 4. The wind came in

hard, around 150 miles an hour, and the Gulf came in behind it, pushing water ashore like it had

been waiting for permission.

Neighborhoods flooded. Homes split open. Businesses went dark. Whole streets turned into

debris fields.

And once again, it was Punta Gorda and Fort Myers.

Once again, it was my family's part of the map.

And once again, I was still in insurance , still at my desk, still answering the phone, still

listening to people try to explain the moment their life turned into before and after.

That is how I experienced Ian.

Not through broken windows.

Not through soaked drywall.

Not through that special Florida misery of hot darkness.

Through voices.

Call after call, all day long.

Same shock, different wallpaper.

Water in the house.

Roof gone.

Car ruined.

No power.

No place to go.

Now what?

After a while, the repetition became its own weather system: one storm moving through a

hundred lives, translated into a hundred different voices.

The news showed landfall.

The calls showed what came next.

People tried to sound reasonable while their lives sat in piles at the curb. They apologized before

crying. They explained damage like they were afraid of being too much. They searched for the

right words, as if the right words could make any of it manageable.

Then Joy called.

And the air left the room.

Up to that point, it had been the usual disaster language: damage, loss, next steps. Awful, yes,

but familiar-awful. The kind you can function inside because you've practiced.

Then Joy came on the line, and suddenly this wasn't just a claim.

This was a person at the far edge of herself.

Joy is autistic.

She was alone and frightened and so overwhelmed I could feel it through the phone. Not just fear. Hopelessness. Loneliness.

The kind that makes every next step feel impossible, even the reasonable ones.

Her voice had that thin, fraying edge people get when they're trying to stay in control and losing

ground by the second. I could hear the isolation in it. The exhaustion. The terror of being alone

inside a problem too big for one nervous system.

In that moment, what she needed first wasn't a claim number.

She needed another human being to meet her where she was.

Because sometimes what people are really saying isn't, *My house is damaged.*

Sometimes what they're saying is, *I don't know how to keep going.*

So I did what women do.

What mothers do.

What people with any mercy left in them do.

I reached for compassion first.

Then steadiness.

Then the right words.

Not magic words, because storms don't do magic.

Steady words.

The kind you offer when you can't fix a life in one phone call, but you might keep somebody

from breaking apart before tomorrow.

I slowed my voice down. I made my tone calm before I even knew exactly what

I was going to

say next.

I reminded her where she was.

What had to happen first.

What could wait.

What did not have to be solved in the next five minutes.

I broke the impossible into pieces small enough to survive.

And I could hear her breathing change.

Not all at once.

Not like in the movies.

Just enough.

Enough to finish the call.

Enough to get through the day.

Enough, maybe, to believe tomorrow was still a place she could arrive.

I don't remember every word I said.

That is the strange thing about crisis.

You are not performing wisdom.

You are lending steadiness.

You are offering your nervous system to someone whose own has gone off the

rails.

And for a little while, it worked.

At least until tomorrow.

That is the part the news never shows.

Not just the destruction.

The aftermath that comes one phone call at a time.

The way survival can leave a person standing and still steal their sense of safety.

The way loneliness becomes its own kind of disaster.

I have a nephew in Fort Myers who still doesn't have the wooden floors he should.

That sounds small until you understand what it really means.

Things are still unfinished.

Still unstable.

Still waiting for a normal that has not come back yet.

It isn't about flooring.

It is about living on top of a delay you never asked for.

I know people who lost everything, and I don't mean just things. I mean bearings. Direction. Margin. The sense of what to do next.

Some of them were already living close to the edge before the storm came along and erased what

little cushion they had.

What storms really take isn't always the house.

It's the options.

That is what I kept hearing from my desk.

Where do I go?

What do I do now?

How do I start when everything looks like this?

Years of this, and I still don't have answers that feel big enough. Not answers that match the size

of what has been lost. Not answers that come with a roof attached.

Ian didn't feel like a surprise.

It felt like a reminder.

Comfort is temporary.

Experience does not make you immune.

And the Gulf keeps receipts.

Two years later, it would remind me again.

Louder.

Meaner.

Closer.

When Helene set her sights on my little island and made "manageable" sound
like something I
had said before I knew better.

Chapter 17

When the Bridge Goes Up

Treasure Island gave me eight good years.
For the first time in my life, I lived on my own not reckless freedom, just delayed
freedom.
The kind of breathing room you don't realize you've been missing until you can
finally hear
yourself think.
Treasure Island gave me air.
Salt.
Space.
It reminded me who I was before responsibility became my defining feature.
And it taught me one rule fast:
On an island, decisions have deadlines.
Once the bridge goes up, time's up.
A true Floridian doesn't usually evacuate just because somebody on television says
a storm is
coming. We are raised on spaghetti models and bad forecasts. We have bought
Slim Jims and
bottled water for storms that never materialized, and slept through storms that
did.
So when the news says leave, most of us shrug, check the sky, and carry on.
By the time Helene showed up on the radar, I was deep into my best late-in-life
freedom ,
living alone, on my own schedule, in my own little paradise and like any proper
Floridian, I
kept my evening plans.
Which meant the American Legion.
Post 158.
That night, the TV behind the bar flashed its usual weather drama: angry reds,
swirling cones,
the weatherman in suspenders with rolled-up sleeves pointing at maps like he
personally knew
the wind.
Nobody seemed ready to treat it like an actual emergency.
We had seen too many storms fizzle.

Too many forecasts cry wolf.

A man at the end of the bar lifted his beer and said, "She'll turn."

Somebody else said, "They always say that. They get paid to be dramatic."

The bartender glanced at the screen and said, "Y'all want another round, or you want to start

praying?"

We laughed, because that is what Floridians do.

Casual denial, served cold.

I finished my drink and headed home before the rain started. On the way, I cut over to the beach

because apparently I enjoy adding extra weather to my weather.

And that is when everything changed.

The beach, the surf, the sky , all of it looked wrong.

The water was a dark, moody green, like it had decided to go goth. The clouds were layered and

moving fast, black as coal. The air tasted metallic, like the sky was charging itself.

And the beach was empty.

No people.

No birds.

No tourists lining up for one last *I SURVIVED FLORIDA* sunset photo.

Even the wildlife had better sense.

There shouldn't have been waves like that on Treasure Island's gentle stretch of Gulf beach, but

there they were, rolling in and curling with intent.

Not playful.

Not lazy.

Purposeful.

That's when it hit me.

I needed to go.

Not later.

Not after one more update.

Not after sleeping on it.

Now.

Whatever this storm was, she wasn't coming to flirt. She was coming with a vengeance, and she

looked like she knew my address.

I took a breath so deep it hurt. For one brief second, I thought I might throw up. I almost started

running, which is not something I do unless something is on fire or my phone is at one percent.

I walked faster instead, because panic is rude but pride is stubborn.

When I got home, I stood in the doorway and felt something I didn't expect.

I didn't want to be alone.

That surprised me ... not the fear, but the shape of it. I wasn't picturing windows exploding or

furniture floating through my living room like it had plans. I was thinking about the dark. About

sitting alone in a silent house after the power failed. About being the only heartbeat in the room.

So I packed a bag.

Medications.

Chargers.

A change of clothes.

Keys.

Wallet.

Then I grabbed the thumb drives with scanned photos , years and years of life reduced to

something small enough to lose and too important to leave behind.

Then I looked around at the ordinary proof of my life.

The dishes.

The chair.

The little routines.

And my parents' bedroom suite.

That furniture had been with me longer than a lot of people. It wasn't just a bed and dresser. It

was an inheritance. History with drawers.

I glanced at it and thought, absurdly, *I'll be back in the morning.*

I grabbed my keys because that is what you do when you leave home.

You take the thing that says you can come back.

I did not know then that a key can become a souvenir.

I really did believe I would be back in a day or two.

Tops.

That is another thing island living teaches you: there is a brief window before the bridge goes up

and becomes a verdict. After that, you are on your own. No one coming in. No one getting out.

Just you, the dark, and whatever the storm decides to do.

As the warnings escalated and the sky thickened, I understood the rules.

Stay, and you fight alone.

Leave, and you accept whatever you leave behind.

The furniture stayed.

The dishes stayed.

The chair stayed.

My parents' bedroom suite stayed.

The ordinary proof of my life stayed exactly where I left it, as if I were only stepping out for

milk and bread.

At the last minute, with the bridge schedule tightening and my gut yelling louder than the

television, I did something unfamiliar.

I chose myself.

Not my things.

Not my house.

Not the stubborn version of me that would stay and tough it out just to prove I could.
Me.
And once you make a choice like that , even in fear, even with shaking hands , some part of
you remembers.
I crossed the bridge before it rose and sealed the island off from the rest of the world.
Behind me was everything I thought made up my life.
In the car was an overnight bag.
And under my skin was the one thing the storm was not going to get.
Me.
I never saw my home again the way I left it.
I didn't have a plan beyond drive, so I did exactly that. Palms thrashed sideways like they were
trying to slap sense into me. Locals stood on porches shouting colorful weather commentary to
nobody in particular, because Floridians will narrate a disaster like it is a sporting event.
I white-knuckled down Gulf Boulevard, watching the sky unspool into bruised purple and sickly
green.
By the time I hit the mainland, the rain was coming in sheets so thick I could have used a
snorkel. I pulled into the first gas station I saw, the kind with faded lotto posters and a teenager
behind the counter who had clearly seen worse days than this one.
My hair was plastered to my head. My shirt clung to me like regret. Water ran down my arms
and into my hands.
That kid looked at me and said, "Hurricane snacks are aisle three."
Obviously, he was a seasoned therapist.
And honestly, he was right.
I bought chips and bottled water , balanced nutrition for impending chaos , then sat in my car
with the engine ticking and finally took a full breath.
There is a particular cocktail of fear and relief that comes right after you outrun something
without realizing you were racing it.
Hurricanes will do that to you.

Or maybe it's just Florida.

Helene made landfall on September 26, 2024.

Later, she would be reduced to numbers: deaths, wind speeds, storm surge,

property loss , the

usual language people use when they are trying to measure something that

doesn't really fit

inside numbers.

But that night, leaving the island, I didn't know any of that yet.

I only knew the look of the water.

The emptiness of the beach.

The way my body recognized the truth before my brain wanted to.

I thought I was driving away for maybe a couple of days.

Behind me, Treasure Island disappeared into weather.

And by the time Helene arrived, the bridge was up.

Chapter 18

The Bridge Came Down

After days of anxious waiting, my island finally put the drawbridge down.

That sentence should sound comforting.

It should sound like, *We're going home.*

Instead, it sounded like permission to witness what happened.

Here's the timeline, because islands don't do drama they do deadlines.

On September 24, before Helene ever made landfall, the bridge went up.

Not metaphorically.

Literally.

A steel-arm verdict that turned Treasure Island into its own sealed-off world.

Once it rose,

residents were isolated no easy way in, no easy way out. Just whoever had

stayed, whatever

supplies were left, and the storm's schedule.

Helene came ashore in the wee hours of September 26.

The bridge didn't come back down until September 29.

So when it finally lowered again, what I felt wasn't relief.

It was permission.

Permission to drive back in and see what those days had done.

What I remember first is the quiet.

No music leaking out of bars.

No normal hiss of traffic.

No air conditioners humming.

Just the low crunch of tires on sand that had no business being on a road.

Paradise looked like a bomb site.

No traffic lights. No rhythm. No order. Gulf Boulevard had narrowed into something tentative,

sand piled so high along the edges it barely left room to drive. Even the road looked unsure of

itself, like it was waiting for someone official to tell it what to be.

I rolled down the windows because I wanted to smell the Gulf that familiar briny reassurance

that says, *You're home.*

But the air had changed.

It smelled like wet drywall, seaweed, mangled wood, and everything the water had touched and

refused to give back.

The Gulf didn't smell like the Gulf anymore.

It smelled like damage.

Then I saw the Waffle House.

Boarded up.

Dark.

Closed.

No yellow glow. No clatter from the grill. No smell of bacon drifting through the parking lot like

a promise that civilization was still hanging on by a coffee pot and a short-order cook.

Now listen: Floridians can pretend a lot of things are fine.

We can grill in a blackout.

We can call it "a little wind" while patio furniture launches into the next zip code.

We can turn storm prep into a theme night and throw hurricane parties like weather is a hobby.

But if the Waffle House closes?

That is not weather.

That is prophecy.

Emergency management can keep their cones and categories.

Waffle House is the real scale.

If it's boarded up, society has officially tapped out.

The farther I drove, the stranger it got. Boats sat in front yards along the causeway like they had

parked there politely and intended to stay. Palm fronds twisted into power lines. Pieces of

people's lives waited in wet piles by the curb soaked and unrecognizable, but still arranged the

way we try to arrange grief.

Mine.

Yours.

Keep.

Toss.

Maybe.

And then there was my place.

The front door stuck for a second when I tried to open it, as if the house was considering whether

to let me in.

When it finally gave, sand sighed across the threshold like it had been waiting to greet me.

I stepped inside, and my shoes made a sound I didn't recognize.

Grit.

Damp.

Something soft giving way.

There was sand everywhere.

Not just by the door.

Everywhere.

In corners.

In drawers.

In the seams of my life.

The storm hadn't just visited.

It had moved in and redecorated.

I stood there doing what people do when a room suddenly looks like it belongs

to someone else.

I tried to make it make sense.

My brain did that fast scan okay, that's the wall, that's the table, that's the

couch except none of

it felt right. The line between home and structure had blurred.

Then I heard, "You okay?"

It was Bill from two doors down, standing in his driveway with a shovel like

the state had issued

it to him.

"You made it back," he said.

"Yeah," I said, like that meant something.

He nodded toward my door.

"Sand's in everything."

"I noticed."

He gave me the half smile people use when the only alternative is crying.

"Well," he said, "at least it's beach sand. We paid good money to live with it."

That was the island talking through him.

Humor as oxygen.

Then he lifted the shovel.

"Need help?"

That's the thing about disasters.

Neighbors arrive first.

Systems arrive later.

We didn't clean.

That word is too polite.

We dug.

We shoveled and searched and pulled things apart with our hands, trying to decide what was

trash and what was history.

There is a special intimacy to digging through what used to be your life.

You're not rescuing objects.

You're negotiating memories.

What stays?

What goes?

What are you ready to release, even if you never planned to?

We made piles in the yard like we were sorting through somebody else's belongings.

Keep.

Toss.

Maybe.

Maybe was the hardest pile.

Trash has rules.

Keep has rules.

Maybe is grief with mud on it.

Every few minutes I would find something and think, *Oh, there you are,* as if it had been hiding

on purpose. Other times, I'd open a drawer that used to hold something important and find only

sand, water, and the ghost-outline of where the thing had been.

Then came the moment that hollowed me out.

My mother's recipe box was gone.

Not damaged.

Gone.

Those cards weren't just instructions. They were her handwriting. Her little

notes in the margins. *Add more vanilla.*

Don't overmix.

Her voice still trying to feed us from beyond the grave.

Losing that box felt like losing a language.

That's when the storm stopped feeling random.

It wasn't just taking objects.

It was taking continuity.

And in the middle of all that digging, kindness kept interrupting the ruin.

At one point, displaced, filthy, and not entirely sure what day it was we ended up

at an

unfamiliar American Legion that had opened its doors to storm refugees. Strangers

greeted us

like they had been expecting us.

No paperwork.

No proving anything.

Just open arms, a place to sit, and a cold draft beer the kind of disaster relief

FEMA should really

study.

We talked the way people do after something terrible: too fast, too personal,

skipping right past

small talk into the real inventory.

Where were you?

What did you lose?

Are you sleeping?

Are you okay?

No, really?

That is the strange efficiency of trauma.

It can make old friends out of strangers in under ten minutes.

Then, back outside on another street, people walked around handing out peanut
butter and jelly sandwiches and fresh fruit.

Such a little thing.

Bread.

Peanut butter.

A banana.

And it still brings tears to my eyes.

After a storm, even a sandwich can feel like proof the world hasn't completely
given up on you.

Later, I stood in a food line with people whose last names I didn't know,
swapping stories none

of us would normally tell, while the National Guard loaded FEMA water and
MREs into my

trunk.

They offered tarps, toiletries, and flip-flops which sounded ridiculous until I
remembered this

was Florida, where flip-flops qualify as formalwear.

That is the math of disaster:

Ruin on one side.

Ridiculous kindness on the other.

By then, time had gone strange. Hours passed. Maybe days. The sun moved
across the sky like it

was happening to somebody else.

And after the shovels and the piles and the endless decisions, there came a
different kind of

silence.

Not the fearful kind.

The settled kind.

Life shrank fast.

Fewer clothes.

Fewer choices.

Fewer places to put things.

At first, it felt temporary like camping inside my own life, like someone would

hand me my normal back once the paperwork cleared.

But the days passed, and I noticed something unexpected.

I wasn't reaching for much.

I didn't miss the volume.

I didn't miss the excess.

I didn't even miss the constant deciding.

The emptiness made space.

Not just in the rooms.

In my head.

I realized how much of living is maintenance caring for things, organizing

things, protecting

things, moving things from one side of the room to the other and calling that

progress.

Once the things were gone, the care returned to where it belonged.

To me.

And here is what surprised me most:

I was still standing.

I slept fine.

I ate simply.

I woke up and made decisions without second-guessing myself.

What I needed fit into small, manageable corners: morning light, coffee, a few

familiar items,

and the ability to laugh when something went sideways which it often did,

because Florida was

still supervising.

There was a strange relief in realizing that if everything disappeared again, I

would still know

how to live.

I had already practiced.

Loss stripped life down to its bones.

And the bones were strong.

I didn't feel deprived.

I felt clarified.

The storm took so much, and in doing so, it answered a question I didn't know I

had been

asking:

How little do you need to be yourself?

Less than I thought.

Later when access tightened again, when the bridge schedule became a puzzle and

a privilege,

when the island decided who could come and who could not, I understood

something I had never

understood at twenty-five, or thirty-five, or even forty-five:

You can lose a home and still keep your life.

You can cross a bridge with nothing but a bag and a choice

and still make it to the other side.

And once the bridge came down, the island started returning things the way

storms do.

Randomly.

Rudely.

Sometimes with a sense of humor.

Chapter 19
The Island's Lost and Found

Storms rearrange things.

Not thoughtfully.

Not politely.

They don't ask where things go.

They decide.

Like a drunk interior designer with a grudge and no respect for property lines.

After Helene, I checked on neighbors. Everyone moved slower, spoke softer. The island smelled

wrong , less like salty Gulf air and more like wet drywall, wet wood, wet seaweed, and that

unmistakable scent of insurance is about to be involved.

Stories were everywhere.

Some heartbreaking.

Some strange.

Some so ridiculous you laughed and then immediately looked around like laughter might be a

code violation.

Debbie, my friend from the American Legion, told me about ninety-year-old Betty Bingo when

the water came rushing into their home. In the middle of the chaos, Debbie got Betty into a chair.

Somehow, that chair ended up on top of the kitchen counter.

With ninety-year-old Betty Bingo still sitting in it while hurricane water pushed through the

house.

A chair.

On the counter.

With Betty Bingo perched like a queen in a flood.

It sounds made up later.

But storms make the impossible feel practical. In the moment, you're not asking
if it makes sense. You're asking:

Will it hold?

Will it float?

Will it buy us one more minute?

Everyone came out safe.

And yet, never the same.

That's the part nobody puts on a warning map. Survival isn't always a clean
ending. Sometimes
your body makes it out, but your brain stays standing in that rising water.

I was one of the few who evacuated, which meant I got to drive back in with the
luxury of
perspective.

Distance helps.

Sleep helps.

Snacks help.

I'm not proud, but it's true.

And I leaned on humor not to minimize the loss, but to make room for breath.

Laughter isn't denial.

It's oxygen.

Once the shock wore off, I started noticing the island's new logic.

It wasn't chaos exactly.

It was editorial.

Like the storm had opinions about my lifestyle and decided to make cuts.

Nothing was where it belonged. My belongings had clearly vacationed without
me. Things I
hadn't seen in years showed up like they paid rent. Meanwhile, the things I used
every day
disappeared completely, as if offended by my dependency.

Then the island started returning things.

Selective things.

Personal things.

Like Helene had taste.

My Carnival cruise sign-and-sail card turned up across the street.

Across.

The.

Street.

It was lying on a neighbor's back deck, the same deck where his boat used to be tied up. At that

point, we still didn't know where the boat had ended up.

That is not wind.

That is pettiness with intent.

It felt like a message:

You're not going anywhere right now, but I wanted you to remember you once did.

The emerald earring was my favorite insult.

That thing had been missing for months, lost somewhere in my own bedroom while I crawled

around on the carpet like a detective with bad knees.

After the storm, it reappeared outside, wedged neatly between patio stones like it had been

placed there deliberately.

I stared at it and laughed, because what are the odds?

The island was running a lost-and-found department staffed entirely by sarcasm.

And my personal favorite: someone found a Bible open to a page that read:

BE STILL.

It had washed up under a mailbox.

If that isn't the Gulf's sense of humor, I don't know what is.

Neighbors swapped storm stories the way people normally swap recipes. One family found their couch doing laps in the pool. Someone else discovered a stranger's framed photos leaning

artfully against their fence, like Helene had taken up interior design.

And yes, there was still the Waffle House.

Closed.

Again, I am telling you: if Waffle House is closed, society has officially called in sick. The rules

are suspended. The adults have left the building.

But then, like the storm wanted to get theatrical, my friend's piano landed in the middle of the

street.

Her white baby grand, passed down through generations.

Not a keyboard.

Not something you can tuck under your arm.

A full piano.

Heavy.

Wooden.

Absurd.

It sat there on the asphalt like the island had decided we all needed a centerpiece.

Dr. Rhonda walked out, took one look at it, and let out the kind of sigh you only earn after

decades in Florida.

The sigh that says: I am too tired to be surprised.

She didn't scream.

She didn't cry.

She didn't ask how.

She walked right up to it like it belonged there, sat down in the damp air, and started to play.

At first, the music sounded waterlogged: keys sticking, notes a little off, like even the piano was

still in shock.

But Dr. Rhonda wasn't.

Her hands found the rhythm before the instrument did.

And somehow, that was enough.

People started gathering.

Neighbors.

Strangers.

Whoever had been shoveling within earshot.

Someone stood there holding a trash bag full of wet clothes like they had
forgotten why they
were carrying it. A man in work gloves wiped his face with his forearm and
pretended the moisture was sweat.

We stood in the middle of the street listening, because what else do you do
when a hurricane
drops a piano in the road and your neighbor answers with a concert?

For a few minutes, nobody was sorting debris.

Nobody was arguing with insurance in their head.

Nobody was trying to make the loss add up.

We were just there.

Together.

When she finished, there was a beat of stunned quiet.

Then somebody clapped.

Then everybody clapped.

Not polite applause.

Real applause.

The kind you use when you don't have words but still need to say something.

Dr. Rhonda stood up, gave a little bow like it was Carnegie Hall, and said,

"Well. Might as well
use it before it swells."

That was the moment I knew the island was going to survive.

Not because the houses would all be fixed quickly.

Not because insurance would become efficient.

Not because permits would rain down from heaven, though wouldn't that be a

nice little weather

event.

But because people were still people.

Still ridiculous.

Still generous.

Still capable of making something out of almost nothing.

Helene took a lot.

But she also left reminders, out of order and out of context, that life doesn't

become meaningless

just because it becomes unrecognizable.

A cruise card across the street.

An emerald earring between patio stones.

A Bible under a mailbox.

A piano in the road.

A woman playing it anyway.

And out there beyond us, already gathering itself, was Milton.

Chapter 20
Real Housewives of Hurricane Season

Kevin Jr. comes with attitude, yes but also with strength, comfort, and a get-it-done energy that steadied me more than he probably knew. I leaned on him and caught my breath.

For the next two weeks, I drifted in shock, couch-surfing from one place to the next like a

woman starring in a disaster-themed remake of *The Bachelorette* except the rose ceremony was

just me deciding which blanket smelled least like a dog.

Most nights, I'd wake up at 2 a.m. with my brain doing inventory before my eyes even opened.

Okay.

Whose living room?

Which ceiling fan?

What is that sound?

Is that a cat judging me?

Trauma does that.

So does sleeping in somebody else's throw pillows.

Right after Helene, I stayed with my friend Dawn four women, one elderly person, and one

toddler in a house that quickly became a full-contact sport. There is no spiritual growth quite like

trying to process catastrophe while a toddler is thrilled by every cabinet and an older woman asks

where the remote went for the third time like it's a federal investigation.

Then there were a few blurred days of borrowed couches and borrowed quiet, and at one point

maybe even my car pathetic and, honestly, wildly efficient.

That stretch is fuzzy now, but my body still remembers it. Every so often, I still wake up

disoriented for half a second and think:

Whose couch is this?

Thirteen days after Helene, just as I started to catch my breath, Hurricane Milton came barreling straight at us.

Not at the island this time.

At the inland couch I was borrowing at my son's place, far from the Gulf.

Of course it did.

Because in Florida, you don't just get one storm.

You get a sequel.

And the sequel is always louder.

I kept thinking:

Please. Not again.

We evacuated again, and this time it was weirdly simple: grab an overnight bag, toss supplies and the dogs in the car, and go.

When everything you own fits in a backseat, evacuation becomes efficient.

The emotional weight is heavy.

The packing list is merciful.

Evacuating with millions of other Floridians, though?

That is something I never want to repeat.

I-75 was bumper-to-bumper from Tampa to Atlanta every lane packed, including the shoulders.

Hazard lights blinked like a second skyline. Gas stations had lines like theme parks, except

nobody was smiling and the ride was just anxiety.

And the sound tires grinding the shoulder for miles got into your bones.

It wasn't traffic.

It was a migration.

A whole state quietly deciding, *Nope.*

Somewhere north of Tampa somewhere that should have taken forty minutes and took forever

we pulled off for gas.

The station was chaos under fluorescent lights. Cars parked at angles that
suggested everybody had abandoned geometry. People stood in lines curling
around the building, clutching beef jerky and bottled water like they were
currency. The pumps beeped and clicked and shut off early like they were tired
too.
A man near us kept refreshing his weather app and muttering, "It moved
again," like he was
tracking a cheating spouse.
A woman in a minivan held a crying toddler and whispered, "Mama's got you,"
while staring
straight ahead like if she blinked, she might lose her nerve.
When it was finally our turn, the pump stopped at a number that felt insulting.
Kevin stared at it like it had personally betrayed him.
"That's all?" he said.
"That's all," the guy at the next pump answered without looking up, like we
were all in the same
support group now.
We got back on the road with half a tank and a full-body ache, and nobody said
what we were all
thinking:
If this keeps going, what do we do?
When Milton made it clear this was not a drill, we did what any sensible group
of displaced
Floridians would do.
We caravanned to Atlanta.
With nowhere else to go, we aimed for my other son's one-bedroom, one-bath
apartment and
called it a plan because "plan" is what you call desperation when you are trying
to stay polite.
For the next week, five adults, one teenager, two dogs, and two cats lived
together like a reality
show nobody auditioned for. If Bravo had found us, they would have called it
Real Housewives
of Hurricane Season and filmed it in one continuous shot.
We tried not to talk about why we were suddenly "vacationing" in Georgia,
because saying it out
loud felt like tempting fate.
Instead, we focused on logistics.
There was a bathroom line.

There was kitchen choreography hip checks, apologies, the occasional passive-aggressive sigh.

We played *Whose Coffee Cup Is It Anyway?* because in a one-bedroom apartment, every mug

looks innocent until it isn't, and nothing starts a fight faster than touching the cup somebody has

emotionally bonded with.

We took turns walking the dogs, stepping over air mattresses and emotional-support duffel bags.

Sleeping arrangements were decided by drawing straws, which sounded democratic until you

lost and discovered democracy still meant the pullout couch.

On the third night, I woke up at 2 a.m. to the sound of someone moving around in the kitchen.

For a second, I didn't know where I was. The ceiling looked unfamiliar. The room smelled like

somebody else's detergent and dog. Somewhere in the dark, an air mattress gave that small

rubbery sigh it makes when somebody rolls over.

I padded into the kitchen.

My son was standing at the counter with a glass of water, the light from the stove clock catching

one side of his face. He was staring out the window like he was listening for something or maybe

listening for the absence of something.

"You okay?" I whispered.

He nodded without conviction.

"Just… awake."

We stood there in that tired midnight silence refrigerator humming, dogs finally quiet, the whole

apartment holding its breath.

Then he said, "Mom, I'm glad you're here."

It cracked something open in me.

Because I was glad too.

Glad to be with my kids.

Glad we had gotten out.

Glad we were still breathing.

And also furious that getting out had become necessary again.

I squeezed his shoulder and said, "We're fine."
It was a lie and a prayer, the two things mothers say most often in a storm.
Atlanta called us evacuees.
Not refugees, even though that is exactly how I felt.
Southern hospitality showed up everywhere, but exhaustion came with us.
We noticed the
NO VACANCY signs immediately
 Every hotel looked full smug, even.
Thank God for one-bedroom apartments and sons who answer their phones.
Without that, we might have been sleeping in the car under a Waffle House sign, which felt
dangerously on brand.
Somehow, people could tell we didn't belong our tans, our flip-flops, the way we kept checking
hurricane updates in a city that wasn't even raining.
Or maybe it was the look in our eyes:
The vacant stare of people who left home without knowing whether home would still exist.
But even through the haze, people were kind.
"Y'all okay?" became the citywide greeting, asked gently, like they already knew the answer.
One day at Kroger, the bagger made us out as Florida evacuees immediately. I tried to slip him a
tip, and he refused it kindly.
Right there by the carts and sliding doors and stacks of weekly circulars, he asked if he could
pray for us.
So I stood under fluorescent lights holding a bag of groceries while a stranger asked God to keep
us safe.
That kind of kindness makes you feel held and worn out at the same time grateful, humbled, and
just tired enough to cry in produce.
Inside the apartment, the animals ran their own parallel universe. Annie the Chihuahua self-
appointed ringleader clearly believed chaos was a management style. Nobody ever figured out
who got into the garbage or who visited the litter box, but somehow it all held together: routine,
patience, and a whole lot of love.
And maybe that's what we were doing too.

Stuffed in like sardines.

Nobody bruised.

Everybody still breathing.

We laughed. We played cards and board games. We watched TV.

Against all odds, we mostly got along.

Shared disaster lowers expectations and raises tolerance.

Fear hummed in the background like an appliance you stop hearing until the

power goes out.

Eventually, we were allowed back into Florida.

That's when the "vacation" ended.

The jokes dried up.

We packed the air mattresses, gathered the animals, and got back in our cars

heading south

toward whatever was waiting.

Evacuation is just a vacation with a return address you're afraid to open because

eventually, the

storm sends the bill.

Atlanta had held us kindly.

Now it was time to face the truth we had worked so hard not to imagine.

We weren't evacuees anymore.

We were going home to find out what survived.

And when Milton finally moved on, we did what evacuees always do.

We drove back toward whatever was left.

Chapter 21

Fear, Confirmed by Measurement

It wasn't easy, but we packed up anyway: bags, leashes, half-finished coffees, and the little

pieces of borrowed normal.

Then we opened the door and headed south, driving straight toward whatever Hurricane Milton

had left behind.

People like to talk about storms as if they are clean facts.

Categories.

Cones.

Wind speed.

Landfall.

As if naming something makes it behave.

Helene hit hard on September 26, 2024 — Category 4.

Milton followed on October 9 — Category 3.

Because Florida offers sequels, and nobody asks if you want the director's cut.

You can laugh in the shelter. You can white-knuckle the evacuation. You can sleep on

somebody's pullout couch and call it "fine" because the dogs are quiet and nobody is actively

crying.

But the drive home is where the truth gets loud.

That drive is mostly a blur now highway, brake lights, updates, the same prayer in different fonts

but I remember the feeling.

Bracing for a picture my mind refused to finish drawing.

I already knew I had nothing normal to return to on the island. My little chapter of freedom was

gone as I had left it. I had made peace with that as much as a person can.

Or at least I had shoved the grief into a box labeled **Later** and taped it shut.

But my son's home?

That was different.

Not because I loved my place less.

Because a mother's brain isn't built for drywall.

It is built for safety.

When we pulled up, the house was still standing.

Mom brain: *Thank God.*

Adjuster brain: *Don't trust the first look.*

Then I stepped out of the car, and my body said it before my mind could:

Something's off.

The air smelled like damp insulation sour and faintly sweet, like wet cardboard trying to pass as

fine. Subtle damage is rude that way. It doesn't announce itself.

It just starts working overtime.

My son came onto the porch looking wrecked in that post-storm way: too much adrenaline, too

little sleep, one eye still on the sky even when the sky was blue.

"Hey, Mom," he said.

"Hey," I said.

I was already scanning the trim, siding, roofline.

Mom brain wanted to hug him.

Adjuster brain was checking for damage.

Inside, the living room looked mostly fine if you didn't know what to look for.

But I knew.

A baseboard with the slightest ripple.

Drywall near a corner that felt soft when I pressed it, like it sighed under my fingertips.

A faint slant in the floor not enough to see, but enough to feel.

That's what scared me.

Not dramatic destruction.

The intimate kind.

The kind your body recognizes before your mind has a label for it.

Outside, the evidence got louder.

The tin carport roof had peeled backward like it tried to escape and got dragged back by gravity.

Shingles were missing in a way that suggested they had left without notice. Holes were punched

clean through metal like something had been sucked into the sky and returned with a grudge.

Not wear and tear.

Airborne debris with commitment.

I walked the yard slowly, pointing things out like I was narrating a documentary nobody had

asked to watch.

"That's a projectile," I muttered at one puncture. "That's not age. That's violence."

My son watched me, then let out a breath.

"So," he said, "it's bad?"

I softened my voice.

"It's real," I said. "Which is different."

Because bad is emotional.

Real is actionable.

And the split is where I live.

The mother in me wanted to comfort him.

The insurance woman in me wanted to prepare him.

Neither one was wrong.

I could already see what he couldn't yet: the calls, the forms, the inspections, the waiting. The way a storm keeps taking long after the wind stops.

Reconstruction had to begin.

And reconstruction means insurance.

Which means you can lose your mind twice:

Once in the storm.

And once on hold.

So we started the ritual.

Photos.

Notes.

Measurements.

Lists.

Damage translated into the driest language possible because anything softer would break.

Meanwhile, the house kept talking in small clues.

A door that didn't sit right in its frame.

A seam where the wall and ceiling seemed to be having a quiet disagreement.

A window that looked normal until you opened it and felt the hitch.

Mom brain kept hoping.

Adjuster brain kept building the case.

Weeks later, possibly months later, time works differently in insurance land, the adjuster who

could actually approve money finally arrived.

I had been waiting for him the way people wait for a verdict.

He stepped out with a clipboard and that careful posture people get when they are walking into

somebody else's disaster. He scanned the roof, paused, and nodded once.

"Tornado," he said.

I didn't flinch.

"Yes," I said, like we were discussing brunch.

He walked the perimeter, taking photos, scribbling notes, then moved toward the foundation. That's when the room inside my chest went quiet.

He crouched.

Measured.

Stood.

Measured again.

My son and I watched him without speaking.

Then he straightened and said, almost casually, "House shifted."

My son spoke first.

"How much?"

The adjuster checked his notes.

"About an inch."

An inch. *welcome to a whole new level of paper work.*

Which doesn't sound like much unless you've ever owned a house, filed a claim, or had a

nervous breakdown near a level.

An inch is the distance between *probably fine* and

Apparently, the house had briefly auditioned for The Wizard of Oz, lifted itself, considered relocation, and decided Florida was already weird enough.

My son blinked.

"An inch?"

"Yes, sir," the adjuster said, like he had just informed us we were low on printer paper.

And there it was.

The thing my body had known before my mind could prove it.

The slant.

The softness.

The smell.

The unease.

Fear, confirmed by measurement.

That is what this chapter of life felt like.

Not panic.

Not chaos.

Something colder.

A forensic examination of dread.

I'm grateful we evacuated.

Truly.

But there is a small, petty part of me that wishes I had seen the exact moment

the house tried to

go full Dorothy.

No ruby slippers.

No flying monkeys.

Just a tin roof, airborne shingles, and a house that said, *Absolutely not,* then set

itself back down.

In the end, it didn't give in.

It took a beating and stayed put.

Much like the family tied to it bruised, displaced, still standing, waiting for the

insurance check

to arrive sometime between now and the next weather event.

We had crossed back into the place where decisions have deadlines.

But this time, the deadline wasn't whether to leave.

It was whether we could keep waiting without losing ourselves.

Because after the wind, after the water, after the evacuation and the return,

there is always

another storm.

The one made of paperwork.

Chapter 22

Pending

More than eighteen months after Hurricanes Helene and Milton, my mind has

finally cleared enough for the truth to land.

I wasn't in denial.

I was in survival mode.

Survival is efficient. It doesn't ask how you feel. It asks what's next. It is basically

a project

manager with no empathy and a color-coded spreadsheet.

What came next was couch-surfing.

And then came the strange part:

Stopping the couch-surfing and still not feeling housed.

For a while, my life fit into overnight bags. Before that, it fit into other people's

living rooms

Dawn's, Lynn's, maybe even the front seat of my car for a night, though memory

and exhaustion

have started sharing a lease.

My body hasn't forgotten it.

Every now and then, I still wake up for half a second, disoriented, thinking:

Whose house is this?

Now the bags are mostly unpacked.

But the feeling hasn't caught up.

For these past 18 months I've lived in someone else's house. I'm grateful. I am.

But I move through it like a visitor.

I don't leave things out.

I don't spread.

I don't settle.

My life stayed in the margins.
There is a particular kind of careful you become when you are borrowing space. You wipe the
counter twice. You rinse your coffee cup until it is spotless. You fold your blanket too neatly,
like tidiness might make your presence less… present.
In the morning, I would make my coffee and stand in the same spot facing the same window,
because routine is the closest thing to ownership. I kept the important things together: keys,
phone, charger, as if I were still evacuating.
Like any moment someone might say, *Okay, time's up*, and I'll have to scoop my life back into a
bag.
The funny part is, nobody is saying that.
My nervous system is.
One afternoon, I almost unpacked.
I took my jewelry out and set the organizer on the dresser. I lined up toiletries in the bathroom. I unscrewed the lotion cap.
 I put my toothbrush in the cup like a woman planning to stay.
Then I just stood there looking at it.
A few minutes later, I put the jewelry back in the bag. I zipped the toiletries into their case. I left
the counter bare again.
It felt like too much commitment.
That's what limbo does to you.
It turns ordinary acts into negotiations.
My son's home is still unfinished.
My Treasure Island place still stands empty and untouched no repairs, no progress. Just a
structure paused in time, waiting on decisions, money, permits, and somebody else's signature.
It exists.
But it doesn't live.
It is like a museum exhibit called **This Is Where She Used to Be.**
Open daily.

Guided tours not available.

That's the part nobody prepares you for. Disasters don't always end with rebuilding.

Sometimes they end with waiting.

And waiting has teeth.

In limbo, the days don't feel dramatic. They feel repetitive. Phone calls. Voicemails. Hold music

that starts to sound like a threat.

Your claim is important to us becomes a line you hear so often it starts to feel passive-aggressive.

Some days, the only thing that happens is an email asking you to upload a document you already

uploaded last month.

Some days, I refill my pill organizer, get nothing solved, and wipe down a kitchen counter that

isn't mine.

That's what I mean when I say storms don't always end when the wind stops.

Sometimes they just put on office clothes.

The grief arrived without hysteria.

Panic burned off and left clarity behind.

I wasn't mourning objects so much as what they held.

Evidence.

Anchors.

The quiet proof that I had come from somewhere and belonged to something.

Photo albums.

My mother's recipe box.

Ordinary things you don't notice until they are gone and then you realize they had been holding

you up like unseen hands.

But I also started noticing what hadn't been taken.

I still had my judgment.

My ability to assess and adapt.

My dry sense of humor.

My will.

Resilience doesn't always roar. Sometimes it takes inventory:

What's left?

What still works?

What still matters?

And sometimes it looks around and says, very calmly:

Okay. So we're doing this again.

Like Florida is a lifestyle choice and not a hostage situation.

When everything external disappears, you learn something precise about yourself: whether your

strength lived in drawers or in your bones.

Mine was still with me.

I didn't endure because I'm extraordinary.

I endured because I'm practiced.

Life had trained me long before the water arrived. I knew how to begin again without drama.

How to accept loss without letting it write the ending.

If there were a continuing education course in starting over, I would have earned the certificate

and the tote bag.

And here's the part that surprised me: my small proof-of-life moment:

One morning, I realized I had stopped flinching when my phone rang.

For months, every call felt like it might be bad news or no news, which is sometimes worse.

Every unknown number made my stomach drop. Every voicemail notification felt like a verdict.

Then one day, the phone rang, and I just answered it.

Calm.

Present.

Like a person standing inside her life instead of waiting outside it.

That's when I knew something in me had shifted.

Not the situation.

Me.

Home, these days, is still a complicated word.

Right now, it means the drawer where I keep my charger. The mug I reach for

first. The corner

where I put my shoes every night.

Small claims.

Temporary borders.

Enough, for now.

Treasure Island gave me freedom.

The storms took the proof of it.

But they didn't take the part of me that knows how to keep going.

And here is the truth that took me a year to admit:

The storms didn't just take my things.

They handed me a second full-time job...waiting for permission to resume my

own life.

So this is where I live at the moment:

Between addresses.

Between decisions.

Between the life I lost and the one that hasn't quite reopened yet.

Pending.

Like paperwork.

Like repairs.

Like a woman with her jewelry still in a bag.

And the thing I miss most isn't the big stuff.

It's the small, ordinary life.

The coffee in my own kitchen.

The chair where I knew how to sit.

The careless freedom of leaving something on a counter because the counter

was mine.

A door I could close without feeling like a guest.

A room that held my history without asking me to explain it.

That is what I want back.

Not everything.

Not the whole old life exactly as it was.

Just a place where my nervous system can stop packing.

A place where the jewelry can come out of the bag.

A place where ordinary can find me again.

Because after all the wind, all the water, all the paperwork, all the waiting, that

is what home

really is.

Not proof that nothing bad happened.

Proof that something good can begin again.

And I am ready for ordinary.

I have earned ordinary.

Possibly with continuing-education credits.

Chapter 23
My Small, Ordinary Life

What I miss isn't some big, poetic idea of home.

I miss my small, ordinary life.

I miss my bike rides the weekly grocery run I treated like church, except with coupons and a

faint smell of sunscreen. I miss planning it around the weather like that mattered. I miss the click

of my bike lock, the heat rising off the pavement like a personality, and pedaling down Gulf

Boulevard with a list in my head and no fear in my chest.

Like the biggest decision of the day was whether I could justify buying peaches and ice cream in

the same trip.

For the record, I could.

I miss riding to the American Legion and locking up my bike like I'd be back in a little while.

Because I always was.

I miss the early beach walks most of all the ones before the tourists fully woke up, when the sand

looked untouched and the birds were busy with their own mysterious little jobs. I'd walk slowly,

listening, scanning for shells that looked like no human hand had gotten there before mine.

And when the walk was done, I'd wander over for a Bloody Mary with good friends the kind of

morning that asks nothing from you except that you show up and enjoy being alive.

I even miss the dumb parts.

Like the time I rode my bike home from Publix in a full-blown cats-and-dogs downpour,

pedaling down Gulf Boulevard like I had personally offended the sky. The rain came down so

hard it felt like it was going up my nose instead of down my face.

The grocery bags were dissolving.

I was dissolving.

My dignity had already called ahead to say she would not be joining us.

I kept pedaling anyway, because that's what you do when you are committed to a bad decision. By the time I got home, I was so wet I could have been returned to the produce section with a sticker.

That was the life I loved.

Not glamorous.

Not impressive.

Mine.

And somewhere along the way, it stopped being routine and became something else.

Belonging.

One morning, I rode out for coffee same route, same stop, same wave to the man who always

swept sand off his walkway like it was a competitive event. A neighbor I only knew as the lady

with the perfect porch plants looked up and said, "Well, there you are. Haven't seen you in a

couple days."

Just like that.

Casual.

Friendly.

Certain.

Not *Where have you been?* like an accusation.

More like: *You're part of this. We clock you. You count.*

I laughed and told her I had been busy, because that's what you say when you don't want to

explain your whole heart before nine in the morning.

But that tiny comment warmed me all day.

Because being known is a kind of shelter.

And then there was the night I was walking home from the Legion, passing Super Scoops my

favorite ice cream place right by the Waffle House, headed toward the Thunderbird, that iconic

late-1950s hotel sitting on the beach like it had been watching people come and go for decades.

A young man about the same age as my boys stopped me. He told me and his friends that I
looked good. That I walked like a boss. Like I owned the island. Of course, I said I do!
We laughed, talked for a minute, and kept going.
He had no idea what he had just done.
He made my whole week.
That night I walked home taller, proud to belong to a place that let me feel seen, not just older.
That's the part that is hard to explain: Treasure Island didn't just give me a place to live.
It gave me back a version of myself.
It gave me a place where my family and friends could come and just be.
Visit.
Relax.
Vacation.
And every night, I got to watch the sunset over the Gulf like it was a personal reward for making
it through the day.
Some nights, it was soft pink watercolor.
Some nights, it was orange and loud, like the sky was showing off.
And I'd sit there, sometimes alone, sometimes with friends, and feel my shoulders drop.
No bracing.
No scanning.
Just that slow exhale you don't realize you have been holding for years.
The Gulf would look calm, polite, almost innocent.
And I would let myself believe it.
When winter set in up north, they came friends from high school, my best friend from
Minnesota, my boys for the weekend bringing jackets they didn't need and stories they did.

We'd sit outside after dinner, the air warm, the cicadas loud, somebody

laughing at something stupid, and I'd look around and think:

This is it.

This is the life.

This is the part I didn't know I was allowed to have.

It wasn't just paradise.

It was proof.

Proof that I could build a life that fit me.

Proof that joy doesn't have an expiration date.

Proof that ordinary happiness counts.

That's what I miss.

Not luxury.

Not square footage.

Not a polished fantasy.

I miss my routes.

My rituals.

My ordinary freedoms.

I miss my refrigerator. My shower. My sink full of my mess the quiet proof of a

life that was

allowed to take up space.

More than a year later, I'm still displaced still carrying my days like they are

temporary, still

trying to understand how a house can exist and a life can be gone at the same

time.

I don't want a new version of things.

I don't want an upgrade.

I want my life back.

My small, ordinary, irreplaceable life the one with the bike rides and grocery lists and bartenders and neighbors and sunsets and easy belonging. The one where I knew the roads, the faces, the rhythm of my own days.

The one where I wasn't just living somewhere.

I was myself there.

I want my fucking life back.

And I'm building it one ordinary day at a time.

The Gulf kept score.

But I'm not going to lose.

I may not get the same rooms back.

I may not get the same furniture, the same recipe box, the same casual confidence of leaving a

coffee cup on my own counter without thinking about it.

But I can still build a life that knows my name.

I can still find a route.

A chair.

A mug.

A morning.

A place to put the jewelry.

A reason to laugh when the sky starts acting suspicious.

That is what storms don't understand.

They can take the proof.

They can scatter the pieces.

They can turn a life into piles marked keep, toss, and maybe.

But they cannot take the woman who learned how to begin again.

Not this time.

Not after everything.

And if you're wondering what comes after a storm like that...

after the wind,

after the water,

after the waiting,

it isn't a neat ending.

It's the part after.

Chapter 24

Full Florida Circle

Life has a strange habit of circling back when you are not looking.

Not neatly.

Not with a ribbon.

More like a cat returning to the exact spot where it once threw up, just to make sure you

remember.

After everything,

the storms, the bridges, the borrowed rooms, the suitcases that never quite got

unpacked, I have bought a house that will finally be mine.

Even now, that word catches in my throat a little.

Mine.

Not temporary.

Not borrowed.

Not a bedroom and bathroom in somebody else's house.

Not a careful little life folded up at the edges so I do not take up too much

room.

A home.

And because Florida is apparently committed to irony as a lifestyle, this new

home is only blocks

from the apartment where my sister Cindy once lived before she made her

journey back to Ohio

to die.

That is what I mean when I say I have come full Florida circle.

Not because life wrapped itself up nicely.

It did not.

Because somehow, after all this wandering, I landed back in the shadow of

someone I loved even

when loving her was not always simple.

Cindy and I did not spend our childhood floating through fields in matching dresses, braiding

each other's hair, and confiding our secrets under the moonlight.

That was not our style.

We fought.

We argued.

We had the kind of sister relationship that could turn hostile over oxygen.

Sometimes she was nice to me, but usually only when Mom ordered her to be.

For instance, one of Cindy's assigned duties was driving me to school. One day, she drove me to

school in her blue Pinto wearing pink furry slippers like that was perfectly respectable driving

attire for a woman in charge of another human being.

Somewhere along the way, she tapped the stopped car in front of us.

Nobody was hurt.

Nothing dramatic happened.

But it was humiliating in that very specific teenage way where you are certain every eye in the

world is somehow on you.

And naturally, this was all my fault for needing to go to school that day.

That was Cindy logic.

If I had not existed or at least had not needed an education none of this would have happened.

As theories go, it was weak.

But she committed to it.

As we got older, Mom and Dad would sometimes travel and leave us alone for days in a house

that was, for all practical purposes, unsupervised.

Those were the parties, I mean, the days when Cindy liked having me around, because I have

always known how to throw a good party.

This was one of my more marketable traits.

Put me in a house with no adults, a few questionable decisions, some music, a fridge full of

things that did not belong to me, and suddenly I was indispensable.

Cindy appreciated me most when I was useful to the social atmosphere.

Honestly, fair.

And that was us.

We were not tender in a Hallmark way. We were not built for soft-focus sisterhood. We were

sarcastic, territorial, funny, annoyed, loyal in sideways ways, and capable of making each other

crazy before breakfast.

But that does not mean there was no love in it.

There was.

It just wore combat boots.

That is the part people do not always understand about family. Love does not always arrive

looking gentle. Sometimes it arrives looking bossy, loud, exasperated, half-dressed, and late.

Sometimes it hands you a ride to school in pink furry slippers and then blames you for the traffic

accident.

Still counts.

And now she is gone.

That sentence is simple, but it does not stay simple when you live inside it.

What I miss is not some polished, saintly version of a sister I never had.

I miss Cindy exactly as she was.

Sharp edges and all.

I miss the private language of us.

I miss knowing she was still somewhere in the world being Cindy opinionated, dramatic, funny,

impossible, alive.

I miss the fact of her.

Sometimes that is what grief really is: not grand sorrow every minute, but the repeated shock of someone no longer existing in the tense you are used to.

And now here I am, after everything, living blocks from where she once lived.

I drive those streets and think about her. I think about how close geography can feel to haunting.

I think about how a place can hold somebody's outline long after they are gone. I think about all

the years when I did not know I was circling back toward this.

It feels like more than coincidence.

Not fate exactly.

I do not trust fate enough to give it that much credit.

But something.

An omen, maybe.

A blessing, if I am in the mood to be generous.

An assurance, on the days when I need one.

Because after the storms took so much, after life got uprooted and rewritten in ways I never

volunteered for, there is something deeply strange and comforting about landing near her again.

Near the memory of her.

Near a chapter of family I thought had already closed.

Maybe this is what family does.

Maybe it does not always save you in the obvious ways. Maybe it does not keep bad things from

happening or make grief more elegant. Maybe it does not even make people easier to love while

they are still here.

Maybe family is simply the thing still under you when everything else gets knocked loose.

The thing you stand on.

The thing you return to.

The thing that reminds you who you were before life started rearranging the furniture.

I do not know what Cindy would say about any of this.

Probably something blunt, unhelpful, and accidentally perfect.

Maybe she would laugh that after all these years, after all my wandering, I still ended up in her

neighborhood.

Maybe she would say, "Well, look who finally made it."

And honestly, I hope she would.

Because for all our fighting, for all the years of being sisters in the most exhausting sense of the

word, I still miss her.

I miss the possibility of growing older with her.

I miss the version of the future where we both made it long enough to become two old Florida

women with opinions, grudges, and excellent stories.

That future is gone.

But this one is here.

And in this life, the life that survived storms, waiting, borrowed rooms, paperwork, grief, and the

stubborn little indignities of beginning again I have found my way back to something I almost

missed while I was busy surviving.

Not just a house.

Not just a street.

A circle.

A family-shaped one.

Maybe this new house is not the ending.

Maybe it is the proof that I am still allowed to begin.

That I can lose one home and still walk toward another.

That I can carry my grief, my humor, my history, my stubbornness, and whatever dignity

survived the couch-surfing years into a place with my name on it.

Mine.

There is that word again.

Small.

Heavy.

Beautiful.

Mine.

And maybe that is the point.

Maybe family is not just who we come from.

Maybe it is what we survive on.

Maybe home is not the place where nothing bad happens.

Maybe home is the place where, after everything bad happens, you still find

yourself standing. And maybe, if you are lucky, you land close enough to

someone you loved that you can almost

hear her say:

"Well, look who finally made it."

Epilogue

The Part After

People love an ending.

They love the version where the house is rebuilt, the photos are replaced, the dog is clean again,

and the woman stands in the doorway of her restored life holding a cup of coffee like she just

won something.

I would love that ending too.

I love closure. I love a tidy narrative. I love when the paperwork is finished and nobody ever

says *additional documentation required* again.

But this story didn't end that way.

It ended with me learning the storm was never the whole story.

The real story was the after.

Not wind.

Not rain.

Not floodwater.

The after.

The after has its own climate: long stretches of nothing, followed by sudden phone calls that

change everything and somehow change nothing.

Email updates written in the language of delay.

Your claim is important to us.

Your claim is still being processed.

Please allow 7–10 business days.

A ridiculous sentence when your life is in pieces.

A storm lasts hours.

Recovery colonizes years.

And the longer it goes on, the clearer it becomes: the storm didn't just take things.

It took rhythm.

It took privacy.

It took the stupid little proofs that a life is yours—your groceries, your bike lock, your coffee

cup, your sink full of your own mess, the ability to leave a toothbrush out without wondering if

you should pack it back up.

It took peace of mind first and left the furniture for later.

That is the theft nobody photographs.

The water leaves.

Your nervous system doesn't.

You learn to live like a guest in your own life. You keep your needs small. Portable. Easy to

move. You become excellent at being "fine."

Which is convenient for everyone else.

And brutal for you.

People like resilience a lot better when it's inspirational and not inconvenient. They like the part

where you are brave and funny and adaptable. They like the part where you say, "We're doing

okay."

They don't like the part where okay is a costume.

They don't like the part where loss turns administrative.

They don't like the part where a woman is still waiting for permission to resume her own life.

But that is where I lived.

Not in the storm.

In the stalled-out, paper-cut, fluorescent-lit after.

There is a certain kind of person who believes human reality should be one hundred percent

logical. They like timelines. Procedures. Forms. Categories. Cause and effect.

If this happened, then that should happen next.

Simple.

But storms make fools of simple.

A hurricane does not arrive in a straight line, no matter how many spaghetti models we watch.

Recovery does not follow a checklist, no matter how many claim numbers get assigned.

A house can still be standing and still not feel like home.

A person can be safe and still not feel settled.

That is the part logic never seems to know what to do with.

For years, I worked around claims and policies and estimates and damages. I understood the

need for order. I understood why systems needed rules.

But I also understood something the forms never could:

A human being is not a file.

A life is not rebuilt by logic alone.

Sometimes survival is not a straight line. Sometimes it is a woman standing in the wreckage with

a claim number in one hand, a broom in the other, and enough nerve left to say:

"Well. I guess we start here."

Because life is not a math problem.

It is a weather event with paperwork.

And still, that isn't the whole verdict either.

Because I watched my sons carry more than I ever wanted them to carry, and I watched them do

it anyway. I watched neighbors become family in real time. I watched strangers show up with

shovels, sandwiches, chainsaws, beer, casseroles, prayers, awkward human kindness that does

not fix everything and somehow helps anyway.

That is what I trust now.

Not systems.

Not timelines.

Not promises dressed up as process.

People.

People who show up. People who stay. People who refuse to let you disappear just because your

address got washed out from under you.

More than eighteen months after Helene and Milton, I still notice the light. I still smell the air. I

still feel my body tighten when the sky changes in a certain way.

That is not weakness.

That is history.

And here is the quiet truth underneath all of it, the reason I can finally write this down:

For a long time, I couldn't look back without crying. I couldn't tell the stories without reliving

them. I kept getting stuck on the same question:

Why me?

I stayed angry at the future that got uprooted and rewritten.

That is what grief does when it has not finished with you yet. It keeps dragging you backward—

back into the water, back into the waiting, back into the life that split open before you were ready

to name what was lost.

But now I can look back and stay in my body.

That may not sound like much unless you have lived outside yourself for a while.

Unless you know what it feels like to tell a story and suddenly be right back inside the room, the

water, the car, the phone call, the waiting.

For a long time, remembering felt like being taken.

Now remembering feels more like returning.

I do not mistake vigilance for wisdom anymore, and I do not mistake endurance for peace.

I know what it costs to live braced.

I know what it does to a body, to a family, to a mind.

And I know rebuilding isn't some pretty montage of paint colors and triumphant music.

It is slower than that.

Meaner than that.

More ordinary than that.

It is making coffee.

Answering the phone.

Buying shampoo like you plan to stay.

Laughing when you can.

Telling the truth when it would be easier to tidy it up. It is living without the

guarantee, and living anyway. Somewhere along the way, the question changed.

Not:

Why me?

But:

Now what?

That is what this story is.

Not a comeback.

Not a lesson wrapped in a bow.

A claim.

Not the insurance kind.

The human kind.

A claim on my own life.

I am not beautifully healed. I am not over it. I am not standing in a restored

doorway holding a

mug like the universe finally got its act together.

I am here.

I am scarred.

I am still waiting on things that should have happened by now.

I am still funny.

I am still building.

For a long while, I lived in somebody else's house, paying rent for a bedroom and a bathroom. I

had a key, but it was not the same thing as belonging.

It opened a door, yes.

But not a life that felt like mine.

Later, I found out I was basically covering her entire mortgage payment, which felt like an

impressively rude little flourish. Apparently when life sees somebody already down on her luck,

it likes to add insult as a service charge.

But even that is not the point.

The point is, I was recovering.

I was finding myself again.

More than that, I was accepting myself.

And now I have bought a house that will be my home.

That word still catches in my throat a little.

Mine.

Not borrowed.

Not temporary.

Not a room I am careful in.

Not a life folded up at the edges.

A home.

When they handed me the key, it felt too small for what it meant.

After everything, the water, the waiting, the paperwork, the rooms that weren't mine, ownership came down to a piece of metal in my palm.

A key.

A small thing.

A ridiculous little object to carry so much meaning.

But there it was.

Proof that I could open a door and not feel like a guest.

Proof that I could put my toothbrush down and leave it there.

Proof that I had not only survived displacement.

I had outlived it.

And none of that is defeat.

Florida will keep doing what Florida does.

The Gulf will keep its receipts.

But so will I.

Weather is strong and unpredictable.

And, apparently, so am I.

You can lose an address and still refuse erasure.

You can lose the proof and still keep the truth.

You can be knocked down, flooded out, displaced, delayed, used, buried in paperwork, and still

remain the one thing the storm did not get.

I am what survived.

I am still my own.

And this time, when I put the key in the door, I am not asking permission to begin again.

I am home.

About the Author

Kathy Porter is a writer living in St. Petersburg, Florida, where the water, weather, and rhythm of island life continue to shape her stories. Her writing is rooted in real life, real loss, resilience, humor, family, and the complicated beauty of starting over.

After years of storms, change, and life pulling her in different directions, Kathy eventually found her way back home to the island she loved most. What once felt temporary, slowly became the place that held her memories, her healing, and the pieces of herself she thought had been lost along the way.

Her memoir writing blends warmth, heartbreak, honesty, and sharp observation, capturing the way ordinary people survive extraordinary moments.
Through hurricanes, family struggles, grief, motherhood, and rebuilding, Kathy writes about the quiet strength people discover when life changes without warning.

The Day My Island Stood Still is both a personal story and a love letter to Treasure Island , the island that never fully let her go.

in the waves
of change we find
direction
SEPTEMBER 27
WAFFLE HOUSE